Qi

Increase Your Life Energy

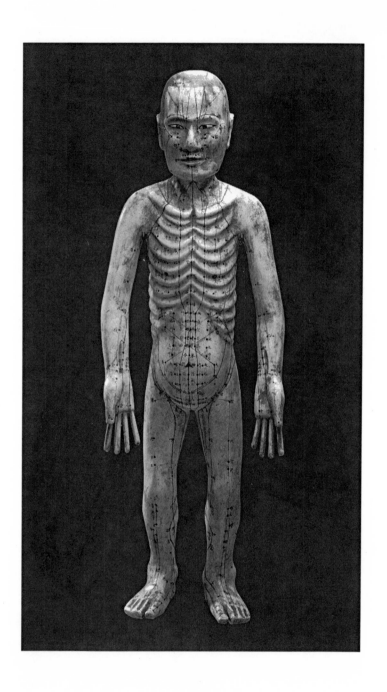

Qi

Increase Your Life Energy

STEFAN STENUDD

arriba.se

Stefan Stenudd is a Swedish aikido instructor, 6 dan Aikikai, member of the Swedish Aikikai Grading Committee, Chairman of the Swedish Budo Federation, and Vice-Chairman of the International Aikido Federation. He is also an author, artist, and historian of ideas. He has published a number of books in Sweden, both fiction and non-fiction. Among the latter is an interpretation of the Chinese classic *Tao Te Ching*, and of the Japanese samurai classic *Go Rin no Sho* by Miyamoto Musashi. His novels explore existential subjects from stoneage drama to science fiction, but lately stay more and more focused on the present. In the history of ideas he studies the thought patterns of creation myths, as well as Aristotle's *Poetics*. He has his own extensive website:

www.stenudd.com

Also by Stefan Stenudd:
Life Energy Encyclopedia, 2008, 2009.
Aikido Principles, 2008.
Attacks in Aikido, 2008, 2009.
Aikibatto: Sword Exercises for Aikido Students, 2007, 2009.
Cosmos of the Ancients, 2007.
Your Health in Your Horoscope, 2009.
All's End, 2007.
Murder, 2006.

This book was originally published in Sweden, 2003, with the title *Qi – öva upp livskraften*. This revised edition is written in English by the author.

Thanks to Tomas Hoffmann and Laila Callegari for their help.

Second edition.

Contents

Foreword 7
Introduction 9
    Spirit and breath 10
    The ether of intention 13
    Let there be 13
    Meridians 14
    Chakra 16
    The Center 16
    The glowing rice field 19
    Spirals 20

Exercises 23
    One snag 24
    Questioning 25
Settings 28
    Place 28
    Time 29
    Dress 33
Posture 35
    Find the right posture 36
    Correct your shoulders 38
    Adjust your balance 41
    Stretch your posture 44
    Sit 45
    Meditate 50
Relaxation 56
    Clench and open 59
    Shoulders up and down 61
    Grimace 62
    Empty gaze 63
    Huddle up 64
    Hang 66
    Rest heavily 67

Breathing 71
    Extend your exhalation 73
    Lower your breath 75
    Belly breathing 78
    Breathe in a square 81
Extension 85
    Gaze 86
    Point 90
    Push 93
    Pull 95
    Grip 98
    Walk 100
The Center 105
    Center breathe in a square 109
    Meditate the center 112
    Sway 114
    Press 117

Chakras 121
    Seven chakras 122

Quick Guide 133

氣

Foreword

I have practiced the gentle and peaceful Japanese martial art aikido since I was a teenager. That is for more than 35 years, and it still inspires me greatly. Something within aikido vitalizes and delights me, just by practicing the movements.

It is *qi*, the life energy. The swirls and spins of the aikido movements stimulate the flow of qi inside me as well as the other practitioners, and whirls through the space between us. Aikido might have the form of a martial art, but in essence it is a way of dancing to the flow of qi.

The word aikido says it all. It translates to *the way of joining qi* (spelled ki when Romanized from Japanese). I let my qi emerge and join with that of my training partner.

In China and Japan, most of the arts – not just the martial ones – are expressions of the qi flow. It is also essential in such healing methods as acupuncture, qigong, and reiki.

The idea of a life energy is present in many of the world's cultures and ancient traditions. It is often linked to breath – as in the Chinese concept *qi*, the Indian *prana*, the Greek *pneuma*, the Hebrew *ruach*, and our word spirit, from

氣

the Latin *spiritus* – also used in the word inspiration. Maybe it could simply be explained as a symbolic way of celebrating the joy of being alive: the breath of life, without which we quickly perish.

This breath of life can be stimulated to increase, and thereby rise to something far more than the mere consumption of oxygen, and extend way beyond the reach of our bodies. That is what the exercises of this book intend. You will definitely feel the difference.

You do not have to believe it to try it. Keep an open but also critical mind, and make your decision afterward. Life is a wondrous mystery. What brightens it up is precious, whether it can be seen in a microscope or not. And you know what Hamlet said to his doubting friend: "There are more things in heaven and earth, Horatio, than are dreamt of in your philosophy."

Stefan Stenudd

氣

Introduction

Qi is the Chinese term for life energy, or life spirit, a vital force that flows through all living things. It is an essential part of acupuncture, qigong, reiki, and the martial arts of the East, among other things. There is no mystery to it.

The nearest western equivalent is probably inspiration. But there is a decisive difference between eastern and western attitudes. Westerners tend to regard this sweet spiritual inebriation as something that either fills us or deserts us, completely out of our control. In the Eastern mind, though, this is something that you can control. You can awaken, stimulate, increase and utilize it, according to your will.

Therefore, this book is focused on the strictly practical aspects of qi: how to get it started and make it grow, and how to use it. Inspiration is yours to call upon at your own wish.

It is not even difficult. The exercises in this book are quite rudimentary, and anyone can do them without effort. Nor do they take much time. There is just one snag: You have to repeat them, preferably every day, and you should do that long enough to establish new habits. It is the only method to make your body act in a way that stimulates your qi, without your mind having to think about it constantly.

You will soon find that life gets another luster. So give it a chance.

Spirit and breath

The word inspiration is directly linked to breathing. It comes from the Latin word for inhaling, which can also mean blowing into something, or even blowing life into something. Its root is the word *spiritus*, spirit, which originally means breath.

Qi, too, is primarily linked to breathing – so closely that it is sometimes difficult to point out their differences. Qi enters and exits the body, like the air does in breathing. And both directions are just as necessary – old qi must exit in order for new qi to enter.

Nonetheless, there is a difference. Although qi can be compared to the air that is inhaled and exhaled, they are not identical.

Qi is more like something hiding within the air we breathe, a necessary essence that the body receives through the breathing. Thereby it is closer to oxygen, the substance that breathing is really all about. The body needs oxygen for its interior combustion, and the oxygen is hidden inside the air. We get new oxygen by breathing in, and get rid of the excess air by breathing out.

If we cannot accept the idea of a so far undiscovered ether as a kind of life force behind the scene, and search for a scientific explanation for the notion of qi, then oxygen and its function seem to be a likely start. Already primordial man must have noticed that breathing is necessary for survival, and that the dead have stopped doing it. Even without a laboratory at hand, our ancestors would have come to the conclusion that there is something in the air that makes us live and walk about.

Already how qi is written in Chinese shows an equal relation to qi and air, as that of oxygen and air. The picto-

氣

gram consists of two parts: one is the sign for steam, and inside of it is the sign for rice. Boiling rice, the basic nutrition for all of East Asia. The body can only digest the rice if it is boiled, and then it is the completely dominating food of the Chinese and the Japanese. It has kept them alive through countless generations. That is life energy, indeed.

When qi is written without the sign for rice, it simply means air. So the complete pictogram points out that the life supporting essence is inside the air, just like oxygen.

Another similarity between qi and oxygen might not be perceived the same by all individuals: Taking a deep breath of fresh air is inspiring, invigorating to the spirit. On the contrary, breathing stale air induces drowsiness and quite possibly a headache. Whether this has to do with oxygen or qi is difficult to say – here they are too closely linked.

A lack of oxygen is sure to bring your mood down, at length even to kill you. That is also said about qi. When there is oxygen or qi in abundance, you get lively and inspired. They seem to do the same, so they may be the same.

But there are differences between oxygen and qi. Although the flow of qi is similar to that of oxygen, it is not equally bound to certain bodily organs. Qi flows in and out of the body, independent of the lungs, the veins and arteries. You can even have a flow of qi when you hold your breath. And qi extends far beyond the body, which is something that the oxygen you breathe is unable of.

So, if you want to understand and try qi, it is important not to get stuck on the thought of qi as nothing but a kind of symbol for breathing. Qi is a unique ether, with only superficial similarities to the air we breathe. The vitalization that qi brings might not be as biologically critical as oxygen, but instead it is infinitely more inspiring.

氣

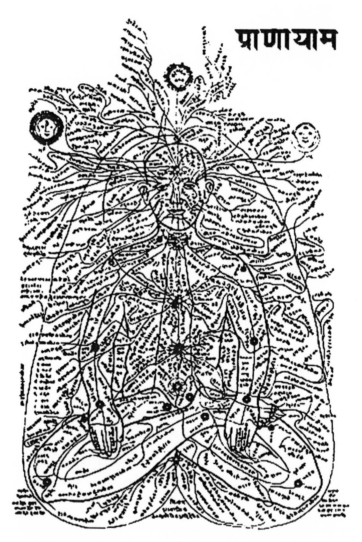

Prana, the Indian equivalent of qi.

氣

The ether of intention

Many would call qi nothing but a thing of the imagination, a misconception belonging to the distant past of man, when countless puzzling phenomena of nature could only be met by guesses and speculation. Maybe it is so – I do not insist on some scientific validity of qi. The question is not even that interesting to me. Whether qi is reality or superstition, it works on what it is to achieve.

A good flow of qi is by its nature healing and wonderfully inspiring. Also, by focusing on the qi flow we can accomplish things that are much more difficult without it, if they are at all possible. Qi does what it should, whether it exists or not.

This points out another similarity – the one between qi and a phenomenon that is well known in the western world: fantasy. Maybe qi is an expression of the power of fantasy. Why not? Still, fantasy is normally linked to dreams and the dreamlike, while qi belongs to being and acting, very much awake. I would prefer to connect qi to willpower and wish. The mental phenomenon that is the closest to qi is intention – when you set your mind to something, or decide to do something.

Qi can be called the ether of intention, a kind of energy by which you accomplish what you set your mind to. Just by directing yourself at something, you get your qi flowing, whether you are aware of it or not. So, it can be called willpower. In the East, willpower is regarded as an obvious expression of qi.

Let there be

In its foremost appearance, qi is the human equivalent of the divine "let there be" by which the Bible states that the creation of the world commenced. In the Book of Genesis, God created the whole world in six days by ordering its components forward: "Let there be light!" and so on. In this mythological primary expression of intention, the universe and life appeared, moving in their intricate orbits and following the conditions of the primordial "let there be" ever since.

氣

God creates light by uttering: "Let there be light!" Bible illustration by 19th century artist Gustave Doré.

氣

A human "let there be" hardly has the same dignity, and is unable that grand scale, but it is still just as fantastic: I am, I look around, and I wish something. We create small things and big ones, news and reruns, artistic masterpieces and catastrophes. In this, we are the image of God: the ability to create.

Without intention, nothing is created. We just vegetate on what surrounds us. When instead – for good or bad – we deal with our reality so that we perceive, approach and transform it, then we are filled with inspiration, and we flow of qi.

Meridians
The Chinese tradition about qi is so old that its origin is unlikely to be dated. By time, it has become a vast and complex doctrine.

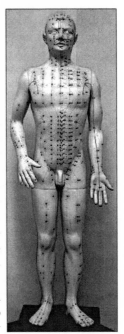

Chinese natural medicine treats the qi flow as something mainly contained within the body, similar to the circulatory system of the blood. The qi equivalent is a number of so called meridians. They are used in acupuncture. Needles are inserted to stimulate points and lines along these meridians, which are meticulously mapped on drawings of the human body, or on acupuncture dolls.

For the purpose of this book, though, the complex patterns of acupuncture meridians are not necessary. Actually, I am in doubt of their relevance – although both acupuncture and acupressure have proven to accomplish quite a lot by using them.

Let us just say that one must crawl before one can walk. The reader who gets a strong and stimulating qi flow

氣

through the exercises of this book, might be inclined to move on by researching the meridians. That is likely to be rewarding, as well.

Chakra

There is one fundamental channel of qi, which can be called a meridian. It has its origin in the Indian tradition that is possibly even older than the Chinese one. India has a concept called *kundalini*, a vitalizing and spiritually refining power that runs from the pelvis up to the top of the head – a vertical line through the middle of the body.

Along this line there are seven *chakras*. The word chakra originally means wheel, and implies rotation. The word kundalini means curled, like a serpent at rest.

The Indian tradition teaches that you can rise from a simple level to one close to the gods, by allowing your life spirit to flow upward this line, through each chakra – to the seventh, the crown chakra, which gives spiritual awakening. The Indian name for the life spirit is *prana*, something that is completely comparable to qi.

The seven chakras and their approximate meanings are, from the bottom up:

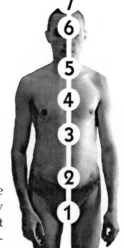

1	*Muladhara*	root
2	*Svadhisthana*	dwelling of the I
3	*Manipura*	city of jewels
4	*Anahata*	unstruck
5	*Vishuddha*	pure
6	*Ajna*	command
7	*Sahasrara*	thousand petaled

The center

Also the Indian tradition has by time become very complex and partially close to impenetrable. But we do not need to get into that either, for the exer-

氣

cises in this book. The very basics, which are the same in India and China, will suffice.

We will use one chakra, the second from below. It is in the abdomen, a couple of inches below the navel, and that is also the position of the body's center of mass. This point works as a center for the qi flow.

To exercise one's qi flow without any kind of center is difficult at length. Certainly, you can get to know qi and make it flow, but without a center you become passive, almost like a victim, and have a hard time using qi according to your own will. It is like being adrift at sea. Intention can be described as a direction, but it needs a source, a starting point. You benefit from placing such a starting point in one of your chakras.

You could actually choose any of the seven basic chakras of the Indian tradition, but the higher up you go, the more difficult it gets for the inexperienced practitioner to feel something substantial. This is stressed by the Indian teaching, which states that the kundalini movement is from the bottom up.

Then it would make sense to start with the very root chakra, called *Muladhara* in Indian, meaning root. It is at the pelvis, where the genitals are. Indeed, it is quite possible to base one's exercises on this chakra. India has a rich tradition of using the force that is the main one being stimulated by this chakra, which is that of sexuality.

It is a powerful way of creating the flow that ignites chakra after chakra along the vertical line. Even those who have never sensed qi consciously can use erotic stimulation to get a strong flow of qi. And the orgasm is a veritable fountain of qi, up the line where the seven chakras are placed. You can feel it clearly if you think about it, the next time you have one.

Still, that is not the method described in this book. It has its advantages, but it is just as easy to get lost in as a method without any center at all. Sexuality is a power with its own cosmology, far from the easiest one to comprehend and control.

氣

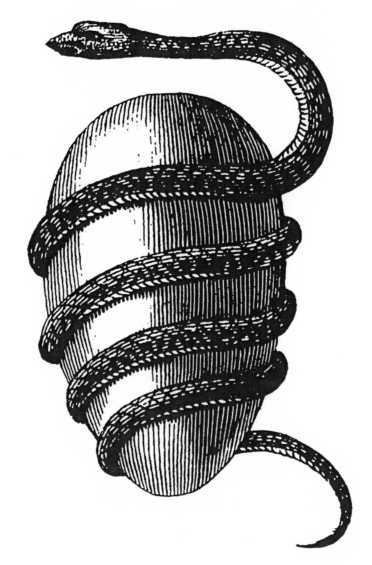

The Orphic egg.

18 Qi   氣

The glowing rice field

The second chakra is called *Svadhis-thana*, which means something like the dwelling of the I. It is primarily connected to having a solid sense of an I, an identity that also includes personal control of it and of how it develops. This chakra is ideal for the one who not only wants to experience his or her qi, but also wants to learn how to control and use it.

In *budo*, the Japanese martial arts, where I belong, as well as in *wushu*, the Chinese ones, this second center is of fundamental importance. That is where you find balance and great power. All your movements should begin and end there.

Also outside the martial arts, this center has vast significance. The painter must move his or her brush anchored in this center. The singer must take the tone from this point, the actor must remain in it to stay believable, and so on. In Zen meditation the hands are placed in front of this center.

The Chinese call this chakra *dantian*, and the Japanese say *tanden*. It is written with two signs, one meaning cinnabar red, and the other rice field. The red rice field. So, rice appears again in connection with qi – this time a whole field of it, and red at that, as if glowing. So the word implies a massive reserve of power, a great resource we have inside of us. That is why the Chinese and the Japanese get their strength from the belly.

It fits particularly well into the exercises of this book, since it also helps with the necessary lowering of your breathing. When starting a strong qi flow, you are supported by the deep kind of breathing usually called belly breathing, or diaphragm breathing, which is also used by opera singers, among others.

You can describe it as a breathing done by the belly, although that is not entirely correct. But for qi training, you

氣

should absolutely think of it as a breathing rooted in the second chakra. It will help you tremendously in getting this deep breathing going, and it will immediately stimulate your qi flow.

Spirals

Kundalini is usually given the image of a curled up serpent. When awakened, it slithers up the vertical line where the seven chakras are seated. The serpent slithers upward in a spiral, not at all in a straight line. The same is true for qi. It moves in spirals, even when its direction is straight. That can be compared to the slithering of the serpent, or for that matter the rotation of a bullet when it leaves the barrel of a gun.

A pair of slithering serpents is found on the *caduceus*, the winged staff that belongs to the Greek god Hermes (the Roman god Mercury). It is sometimes used as a symbol for medicine. In the myth, Hermes threw his staff between two snakes, to stop them from fighting each other.

A more widely used symbol for medicine, also in ancient times, is the rod of Asclepius. It has no wings, and only one serpent, slithering upward. According to the myth, Asclepius, son of the Greek god Apollo, was a formidable practitioner of medicine.

So much in nature moves in spirals, even when the impression is that of a straight line. This is indeed the case with celestial mechanics, the movement of heavenly bodies through space. Galaxies are usually shaped like spirals. Planets and comets move not in circles but in ellipses around their star. And in the microcosm, there is the spiral shape of the genes, the waves of light and sound, and so on. The straight line

Spiral galaxy.

氣

is as rare as it is unnatural in our cosmos. Everything curves, winds, spins, and twirls, like in a joyous dance.

For the exercises in this book, it is not necessary to ponder the spiral nature of qi, but it is good to know. A consequence of it is that recurring movements awaken qi better than solitary ones, and whirling movements stimulate qi more than straight ones. Actions filled with qi contain more movement than what is visible on the surface – much more.

It can be compared to breathing out silently or setting a tone to it – humming, talking, or singing. Qi kind of sings all the time. You can call it vibration. The term is often used about it. The important thing is to see the movement as three-dimensional. It is not only a sinus curve, but the spiral that is the result if the sinus curve is given a third dimension.

Maybe that is why you can get dizzy from an increased qi flow. Dizziness is a whirling feeling, not a linear one. So, dizziness is a very natural state, which can explain why people of all times have been eager to use drugs and other means to induce it. Anyway, qi gives dizziness for free, without any hazard to the health.

氣

Exercises

The following exercises are methodically combined to develop a natural and vitalizing flow of qi. Their order is important, at least to begin with. When you've had some experience with them, it is no longer necessary to stick to the order. You can use your yearning and instinct to choose between them.

You will also quickly notice what exercises you need to continue with, and which ones you can do rarely or ignore completely. You are the one doing them, and for yourself only. Therefore you are the one best suited to judge how they function, and to what extent you need them.

You may also want to modify some of them. That is fine, even recommendable, since it increases your ability to know yourself. But wait with the modifications until you are convinced that you are on the right track. At first, you need to experience how the exercises affect you, what they make you feel. If you hurry to adapt them before you feel how they work, you risk getting lost, and the exercises might cease to function as they should.

氣

The exercises are primarily designed to increase your ability to read and correct yourself. So, listen to how it feels, whatever exercise you do. How does it work, how do you and your body awareness change, what shortcomings do you come across, and how do you progress? You can reason in terms of before and after, like in the TV ads for all kinds of miracle cure products.

At first you will notice a quick change, but then your development will be slower. This does not mean that your ability to improve through the exercises has diminished. Instead, it is your capacity to correct yourself that is sharpened. Your awareness of how much more you can improve increases. Of course, these are important advances, but they can make you feel like you are standing still or even getting worse.

If this happens, consider the before and after. Compare to how it was before you started with these exercises. You will notice that you are always improving.

One snag

These exercises are very effective. You will make noticeable progress shortly. In addition, they are childishly simple. They demand almost no agility, physical strength, good condition, or any other athletic ability. They do not even take a long time to complete. It sounds too good to be true, and of course there is one snag:

You have to repeat them regularly, for a lot of days.

Even if you feel that you have made considerable progress in just a few days, you should not settle with that and stop the exercises. If you do, there is a great risk that you return to square one. This is because the exercises cultivate such basic things as posture and breathing, which have become parts of the everyday behavior that runs automatically, by the autonomous nervous system. You have to establish new habits with how you breathe and what posture you assume. You need new automatics that prohibit the old bad habits from reappearing. That takes time.

It does not help if you do the exercises for several hours

氣

each day, during an initial intense period. It is not even recommendable. A few times in a row is enough for most of the exercises. Persisting beyond that is meaningless. Instead, you must count on needing to repeat these changes of your behavior for months, maybe years.

I dare to claim that it will not be monotonous, since your progress has its own rewards, and they are magnificent. So be patient. Make the firm decision to invest a good portion of your future in this. If you do, the effects of the exercises will be more profound from day one, than if you just felt like testing them a bit.

Questioning

Certainly, you should constantly ask yourself if you find it meaningful to continue with the exercises. You are not supposed to turn into some passive machine. On the contrary, only if you wholeheartedly devote yourself to the exercises will they do their good. If you are doubtful or lose interest, you might as well stop with them.

The aim of all these exercises is to return to the natural behavior, to wake up the inspired entity that dozes inside each of us, after years of misuse. Therefore, the body will feel increasingly liberated, as you work on with the exercises. Your senses will delight in the progress, and each advance you make will feel joyous. Your body will be filled with excitement and long to continue, with the eagerness that children show in front of the cakes in a bakery.

If it does not feel like that, if some exercise is instead uncomfortable and strenuous – then you should take it as a sign that something is not right. Maybe you do the exercise slightly incorrectly, maybe you do it longer and repeat it more often than necessary, or you may have some bodily ailment that complicates matters (although little stands in the way of these simple movements). If so, then try to make the necessary corrections before you continue.

On the other hand: if it feels joyous and liberating, you can just move right on. You do it correctly and have no need of pondering it.

氣

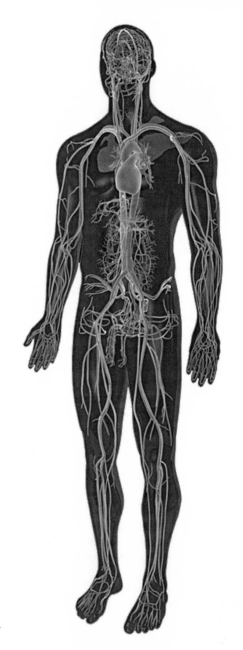

The circulatory system.

氣

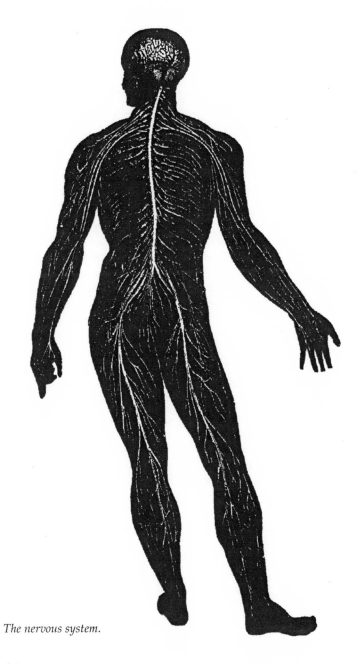

The nervous system.

氣

Settings

The following exercises are simple by nature. Therefore they raise modest demands on environment and other circumstances. You can really ignore the suggestions below, if you find them difficult to follow. But if you do have the opportunity, they are the ideal settings for promoting the very best result of your exercises. I would like you to keep them in the back of your mind, so that you at least adapt to those things that do not cause too much trouble.

You will soon be aware of what details play the most important role in how successful you regard the exercises to be. You should carefully adjust to those circumstances, and the rest you can leave as is.

Place

Of course, a peaceful environment where you are alone and can concentrate on your exercises without interruptions, is the very best place for you to be when doing them. This usually means that you isolate yourself somewhat – indoors in a room that others do not visit, or outdoors on a spot that others do not pass.

Noise is not beneficial, to put it mildly. That goes for visual noise, too – such as flashing lights, lots of movement, or any other muddle of impressions. All the senses should have as peaceful a setting as possible. I am not much for such decorations as incense and soft music – they are widely surpassed by fresh air and silence. A room with stale air, or full of ever so exotic scents, is noise for the nose. Music, independent of the composer's genius, is distracting. You will have a hard time listening to what happens inside yourself.

Nature is no doubt the best environment for anything spiritual, although it is never completely silent or still. If you want to flow of life energy, nothing stimulates you more than having lush meadows as your floor and the sky as your ceiling.

Still, it can be difficult to find a good spot for your ex-

氣

Nature is no doubt the best environment for anything spiritual.

ercises outdoors. You need a place that is not too moist for standing, sitting and lying down, where neither people nor insects bug you, when you have gotten started. Just knowing that you might get disturbed is a distraction.

If so, you had better settle with an indoors environment, although it is less inspiring. It is easier for you to control, so that you can concentrate on your exercises. You may need that, particularly when you are beginning to familiarize yourself with them.

Time

There is really no way of determining what is a suitable time for doing the exercises of this book. Several of them are such that they can easily and quickly be done any time of day. However, to avoid a distracted mind it is favorable to have a time distinctly reserved for the exercises – not one when a visitor or a phone call is expected soon. Nor should you try to make use of a minute or two between one busy moment and another.

The important thing is not to have plenty of time, but to be able to focus fully on the exercises, no matter how tight your schedule is. If you manage to do an exercise in the elevator ride between one crucial meeting and another, then go right ahead. If not, choose your moments more carefully.

In the beginning you may find it tricky to get suitable pauses in your regular life. But soon enough you will notice that your tolerance increases, so that you can do the exercises in not so ideal situations. Maybe you will even be able to use that elevator ride – at least for some of the swifter exercises.

You should not think that you need loads of free time, so that you can work on your exercises for hours. That will only lead to your doing them rarely. Repetition is much more important than length of time. Five minutes a day give much more than three hours once a week.

Unfortunately, I have the impression that repetition at regular intervals is what people find the hardest to accomplish. We are forced to fill our lives with so many annoying and boring habits that we are very reluctant to introduce new ones, no matter how rewarding they are. Make a commitment, order yourself to spend a little time each day for the exercises. If you do not decide firmly, it will probably not happen.

No lifetime contract is needed. Very few people can honor something for that long, whatever the terms or rewards are, so there is no point in making that kind of commitment. But surely you can give it a week? And if that works fine, try another week, and then another.

When you commence with these exercises you will need about an hour if you want to go through them all. But soon enough you will find that you get meaningful results from just five minutes, or even less than that.

Make a selection of the exercises that give you the most. Of course, that may vary from one time to another, according to your needs and your progress.

If you have some self-discipline in establishing these habits, you will notice that they take almost no time at all from your days. The exercises sneak so naturally into your daily rhythm, you stop feeling that they interrupt it. They become one with your everyday life.

氣

When you decide on a suitable time of day for your new habits, there is just one guiding line to follow: Find a time when you have the best chance of doing them peacefully for a while. It can be in the morning, right after breakfast, on your lunch break if you find some privacy, or at night in your bedroom. You know best.

It does not have to be the same time every day, although there is a risk of forgetting your exercises completely if you do not have a fixed schedule for them. Days may pass, when you simply forget. So, I recommend that you stick to a certain time of day – at lest in the beginning. On a day when you are unable to exercise at that precise time, choose another – for that day only – and return to your regular schedule the next day.

If you feel that doing the exercises daily is far too much, also during the first week – then decide for another interval that you can live with. Maybe every Sunday morning? If you cannot put aside time for the exercises even once a week, I doubt that there is much point in doing them at all. In that case, let the book stay on the shelf.

That being said, if you have had an intense initial period of exercises, and they have corrected your posture, opened your belly breathing, and started your qi flow – then it may be enough for you to check yourself by doing a few of the exercises once a week, or maybe just once a month. Finally, it may suffice to do them just a couple of times a year, like when the clock adjusts to Daylight Saving Time, and back again half a year later. Maybe just the morning of each New Year's Day.

氣

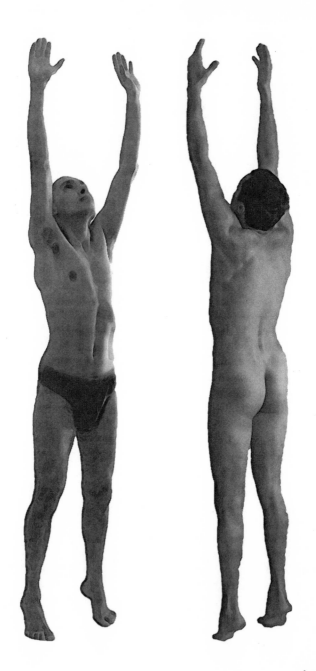

32 Qi 氣

Dress

We have a habit of wearing clothes that are sometimes strikingly similar to nooses on the body – a belt tightened on the waist, a necktie threatening the breathing, shoes that squeeze the feet, sturdy jeans that carve into the crotch, wristwatches restraining the movement of the wrist, and so on.

That is hardly good for any of the body's inner flows, so it is particularly unsuitable when you want to do the exercises of this book. The bodily flows are mainly vertical, and our clothes tend to tighten the body on horizontal lines, so they do indeed become obstacles.

When engaging in these exercises, you need to have loose clothing, and as few garments as possible. No doubt, the best is to be completely nude. Try it sometime, and you will notice how immensely liberating that is to the body.

Even seemingly marginal clothing, like socks or silky soft panties, inhibits the body flows to some extent. That may be so minute, you hardly notice it when you exercise – but it is an obstacle, nonetheless. If you can exercise naked, then do it, at least occasionally. Make sure to try it when you begin to learn this, especially when you exercise relaxation and breathing. Otherwise, be as lightly dressed as possible, and use clothes that are loose and soft.

Really, the only ideal clothing is the one we were all born with.

五脏六腑之图 以下俱杨氏

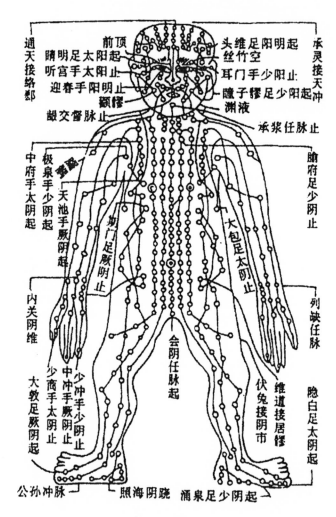

通天接络郄

前顶起
睛明足太阳止
听宫手太阳
迎春手阳明止
头维足阳明起
丝竹空
耳门手少阳止
瞳子髎足少阳起
渊液
颧髎
龈交督脉止
承灵接天冲
承浆任脉止

中府手太阴起
极泉手少阴起
天池手厥阴起
期门足厥阴止
大包足太阴止
臑府足少阴止

内关阴维
列缺任脉

大敦足厥阴起
少商手太阴止
中冲手厥阴止
少冲手少阴止
会阴任脉起
维道接居髎
伏兔接阴市
隐白足太阴起

公孙冲脉
照海阴跷
涌泉足少阴起

仰人经图

Acupuncture meridians.

氣

Posture

For qi to flow freely through the body, it is necessary to have a good posture. Like with a water hose: if it is bent, the flow will stop.

With the water hose as well as the posture, there is a degree of tolerance. The hose does not need to be completely straight in order for the water to run through it with ease, and the body must not be as straight as a pine tree for qi to flow through it. On the other hand – if you want to get a veritable fountain of qi, then the bodily channels need to be straightened, and the posture needs to approach perfection.

When you work on your posture, you will by time become aware of how adjustments so small that they measure less than an inch can still cause veritable leaps in the development of your qi flow and well-being.

Do not bother to be too meticulous at first. That only causes tensions to sneak up on your body unnoticed. But at length, do not settle for anything less than perfection – a posture that makes your body feel like a living pillar between Heaven and Earth, like the mythical pillar that holds up the world.

Man is born with an instinct for the correct posture. When infants learn to walk, they are excellent examples. Their backs are straight, their bellies protrude, and so on. But then we put them in ergonomically doubtful chairs, dress them with clothes that limit their agility, and demand of them to bend for hours over schoolbooks or computer screens. Soon, their good posture is history.

Years later, when they try to reestablish a good posture, they have to counter a long time of bad habits, which have become reflexes. The body has learned a faulty order, and it practically creaks when it is forced to relearn. You can correct you posture momentarily, without too much

氣

trouble, but to get a lasting result and give the body a new habit, you need persistence. Otherwise your body falls back to old ways.

Find the right posture
There is no point in trying to adjust your posture by conscious correction of details – the neck here, the back there, the belly this way, and the shoulders like that. Then you get lost in your body, and new discrepancies replace old ones, in a chain without end. The body knows how it should arrange itself, so it just needs impulses in the right direction. It is really all about releasing the tense habits you have forced your body into, so that it can return to the natural.

This is one way to do it:

1   Lie down on your back, right on the floor. You can make yourself more comfortable with a carpet or a blanket, but not something as soft and thick as a mattress. Absolutely no pillow. The back of your head should rest on the floor in such an angle that the neck is straightened, and your chin closes in on your chest – but not all the way to it. Your arms are extended along the sides of your body. The legs are straight, in an angle that puts the feet at approximately shoulder distance from one another.

氣

2   Rest in this position for a minute or so. Close your eyes, so that you are not distracted by the surroundings. It also makes you more sensitive to how the body adjusts itself on the floor. You should give in to gravity, so to speak, and let your whole body sink heavily to the floor.

3   Stand up slowly. It does not matter how you get up, but do it calmly, without any sudden jerks.

4   Stand with your feet at shoulder distance, and your arms along the sides of your body. Try to *assume exactly the position you had when lying down*. That's the point of the exercise. The good, natural posture is just about identical when lying down and standing up. But do not try to correct some details, once you stand there. Just let the body by itself find the same position standing up, as it had lying down. Let it happen sort of automatically.

5   Remain standing in this position for about a minute, and not much longer. Otherwise there is a risk that you unconsciously start making adjustments of your posture, and they may very well be faulty – or accomplished by some unnecessary muscle tension. Just stand there for a while, relaxing in the position you happen to be in. Feel it. Is it different from how you normally stand, and how your body normally feels? Already the very first time you do this exercise, you are likely to notice that the body feels more at ease, more pleasant, and the posture is more restful.

6   Repeat the whole exercise. *Once is never, twice is always.*

氣

Doing this exercise three times in a row is all right, but no more. Then your conscious mind takes over and complicates things, instead of letting your instinct and body take care of it. It is much better to settle with a couple of times, even if you feel that everything did not get perfect. Instead, repeat the exercise at another time.

•

In the beginning, you should do this exercise at least once a day – even more frequently if you can. Try to do it each morning and evening, so that you begin and end the day with a good posture. Doing it right before you go to bed is excellent, since it stimulates the body to improve some aspects of your posture during your sleep.

By time, when you feel that the corrections this exercise does to your posture are minimal, it will be enough to do it now and then, at increasing intervals. Maybe once a week is fine, and later on just once a month. Should you observe that nothing happens to your posture in this exercise, although you do it as rarely as once a month, then you probably do not need to repeat it anymore. It has given you what it can, and you had better spend your time on other things.

Correct your shoulders

It is common for people of today to have sloping shoulders, from too much deskwork and what not. This afflicts the neck and the whole chest. The above exercise for finding the right posture does not really solve that problem. But this simple method is a good way of correcting your shoulders, unless they are completely straight – and they are probably not.

You can do it after the previous exercise, when you stand up and have rested for a little while in that position. Well, you can correct your shoulders any time you like or feel the need. The exercise works fine on its own. Just be aware that it is hard to correct the shoulders if the back is far from straight. Should that be the case, start with the previous exercise, and then do this one.

氣

1   Stand straight with your arms along the sides of your body, and your feet at approximately shoulder distance. Relax.

2   Extend your arms to the sides, so that they are at shoulder height. Extend your index fingers, too, as if you *point at something far away*. Do not focus on extending your arms from your shoulders, because that can get tense. Instead, concentrate on the fingers pointing far away. Enhance this by glancing in both directions. If you have familiarized yourself with the proper breathing technique, you should make an extended exhalation at this moment, as if you are breathing through your index fingers and your exhalation air is flowing in the same direction you point. Keep this extended position only as long as it feels vivid and comfortable – no more than a minute, but less is fine. It is enough that you feel for a moment that you reach really far.

3   Let the arms fall to your sides and rest there, *without changing the position of your shoulders*. This will immediately make your shoulders feel that they have sort of opened, lightened, and become freer. You might expe-

氣

rience it as a tingling inside of them, a pleasant sensation that tends to spread to the chest, maybe also the neck.

4   Rest in this position for a moment, while noticing how it feels.

5   Repeat the exercise. Once is never, twice is always. You can do it as many times in a row as you like, but I doubt that it makes much difference after the second or third time.

You should make it a habit to do this exercise right after the previous one, as long as it makes a noticeable difference in your shoulders. It helps to improve your posture. You can also do it by itself, without the previous exercise preceding it – but only if it gives an obvious effect. Otherwise it is a waste of time.

It is an excellent stretching exercise when you have sat for a long time by the computer, or worked at a desk with something minute and complicated.

Maybe the shoulders will not open by this exercise, no matter how often you repeat it. Then it can be of additional help to do the whole exercise lying down.

氣

Lie on your back, and extend your arms to the sides, in contact with the floor. After doing the pointing, bring the arms back to your sides. It is almost like making snow angels. If your shoulders have been quite sunken, doing this exercise lying down may be what makes them change into a more natural position.

Adjust your balance
With a good posture you are always in good balance, too, without having to work on it. You are centered – but more about that later. So, by testing your balance you get a method to perfect your posture, which is what the following exercise is about.

It should be done with a light mood, almost indifference, so that you avoid getting tense by thinking too much about details in your posture. Do not try to adjust your body in order to find a perfect equilibrium. Just play with the movements of the exercise, so that the body by itself makes the necessary adjustments. Your conscious mind should not be involved in it. The best is if you are not even aware of the process. So, don't give it much thought.

It is suitable to do this exercise in connection to the first one above, especially as long as you feel that it improves your sense of standing steady. Balance is primarily being able to rest in your posture. When your posture is good, you can feel that all parts of your body have fallen into place, so that you do not need an intricate system of tense muscles to keep them there. It is a natural equilibrium, where the whole body is in balance. It is not stiff at all, but has a soft flexibility that keeps your sense of balance even when you move.

1   Stand straight, with your arms by your sides and the feet at shoulder distance, just like in the previous exercises. Your legs should be slightly bent, which makes them more flexible and springy.

2   Get up on your toes, without changing your posture in any other way. Keep your arms by the sides. Stay in that

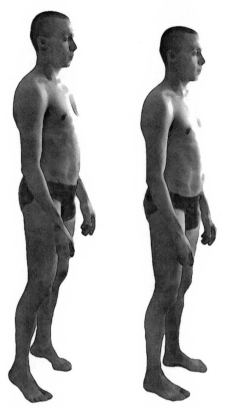

position for a few seconds – just enough not to start swaying or losing your balance. If you lose your balance – do not try to correct your position, but go directly to the next movement.

3   Sink down on the soles of your feet again, still *with the same posture.* Do not change your vertical angle, for example by leaning back more than when you stood on your toes. Otherwise you will put too much weight on your heels, and your knees will have a tendency to lock in a backward position. That makes the whole body stiff and clumsy. Instead, keep your angle, which is probably leaning slightly forward. Check if something has hap-

氣

pened to your posture. If your body is in natural balance, your posture has not changed in the least.

4   Repeat the exercise. Once is never, twice is always. Actually, this exercise can be repeated as much as you like, like pure calisthenics. Still, remember to halt a little while, both when you are on your toes and when you are down, so that you can feel what happens to your posture. It is the short pause on your toes that actually corrects your posture, minutely – but you do better not to think about it.

As I have said above, this exercise makes the most sense if done in combination with the first one, but it can be done by itself as well. It is even a decent replacement for the first exercise, when you are unable to do that one. You may be in a place where you are reluctant to lie down on the floor. This exercise, too, helps to correct your posture, although to a lesser degree than the first one.

You can also test your balance by doing this exercise once, then take a few regular steps forward, stop, and do the exercise again. When you walk, the body posture tends to fall back to old habits, so you might discover that it is like starting over. A balanced posture leads to a better way of walking. This you learn and establish by mixing walking with this exercise of balance. So, do not hesitate to try it as much as you like.

When you find no difference in your posture, whether you are on your toes or not – then this exercise is no longer necessary for you. But until then you do well to repeat the exercise as much as you do the first one, or maybe even more frequently, since

氣

it is so easy to do wherever you are. You can even do it a little at the same time as you stand and converse with other people, and they will not find your behavior that very peculiar.

Stretch your posture

To stretch your body is a natural way of correcting your posture, but also of opening up the body. When you stretch – in

about the same relaxed way as in a big yawn – you will straighten your posture and release some tensions in it, without having to think about it. Your body gets more at ease, your limbs and vertebrae correct their positions, and the inner of your body sort of opens up.

This exercise might as well belong to the ones working on your breathing, but what you should concentrate particularly on is how it gets you kind of taller and straighter. That is why I have placed it in the group of posture exercises.

This is what you do:

1   Stand straight, with your arms by your sides and the feet at shoulder distance, just like in the previous exercises.

2   At the same time as you inhale slowly and deeply, raise your arms, straighten your fingers, get up on your toes, turn your face toward the ceiling, and look straight up. Extend yourself upward in this position, as if your inhalation sort of pumps you up.

3   Start a strong but not hasty exhalation, and *stretch even more upward*.

氣

4   Go down to the initial position, before you breathe in anew.

5   Take a few normal breaths and relax.

6   Repeat the exercise. Once is never, twice is always. You can do it as long as you feel that you stretch more than before. When you do not feel that anymore, you might as well stop for now.

When you learn the breathing technique and extension I present later on in this book, you will notice that this exercise increases in effect and meaning. But already prior to that, it does a lot of good as an introductory exercise of relaxation. You can do the exercise daily, and as many times as you like, but you will soon notice that, properly carried out, it is enough to do it once – or twice, if my frequently repeated motto is to be followed.

Sit

Few things are as damaging to the posture of modern western people as the way we sit. In our chairs it is close to impossible at length to keep a good posture. This is mainly due to the right angle between the legs and the torso, which is so strenuous on the back that it soon bends and tends to remain in that position.

In addition to that, work desks and dining tables and the like are usually so low that you have to bend your back even more. But mainly, we sit too much in chairs – and it is not good, even if we should manage to keep a good posture, which we do not.

There are chairs designed to give a better angle between the back and the legs, making the latter lean downward. But these odd creations have not replaced many normal chairs. Anyway, it

氣

is not possible to sit comfortably in such chairs for long either, and it is more difficult to vary your seated position in them, compared to ordinary chairs. You need to move about, even if it is only in your chair.

Some authors prefer to do their writing standing up. That may be a way of avoiding the seated body's itch to move away from the work place. Ideally, we should have our working stations arranged so that we could easily and frequently switch between sitting and standing.

In the East, people often sit on the floor. Westerners usually find that very uncomfortable. Still, I would like to introduce an exercise of sitting, among those aimed to improve your posture, because correct sitting helps a lot in finding and cultivating a good posture. Try it, even if stiff joints protest. You do not have to sit for long when you do the exercise, and if you persist you will soon be able to do it with greater ease.

You can sit right on the floor, which is kind of rough, but it is also fine to do it on a blanket. You can even fold it a couple of times, to make it softer to sit on. A pillow or a mattress, though, will be too thick for you to find your own balance. Also, on something that is both thick and soft, you sink down and sort of get stuck – often in a bad position of the body that is quite difficult to correct on such a surface.

Make sure not to wear clothes that tighten around your waist, because that pressure is likely to increase when you sit down.

Of course, there are many ways to sit, some better for the posture than others. I would like to divide them into two kinds: one kind is with your legs in front of you, and the other with the legs under you.

The first kind includes such seated position as with your legs crossed, or simply squatting with or without your buttocks on the floor. Regular sitting in a chair would also belong to this category. All these ways of sitting with your legs in front of you are regarded as more comfortable than the other kind, with your legs under you. Still, the latter is the kind I choose for this exercise.

氣

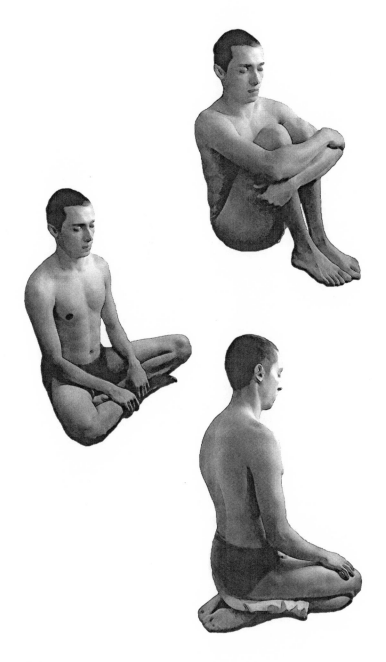

氣   Qi 47

Those of the first kind make it very difficult for you to keep a straight back. The hips tend to tip backward quite forcefully. The second kind, which can really just be done in one way, is such that your back practically by itself assumes the right position. That makes it particularly advantageous when you are about to learn a good posture.

In this way of sitting, your shinbones and the upper sides of your feet are on the floor, your knees are parted slightly, and your buttocks press on the heels, or sink down between them. It is the most common sitting in traditional Japanese culture.

Unfortunately, many westerners are so stiff from a life in chairs that their knees will not bend enough for their buttocks to meet the heels. If that is the case with you, you can put a pillow in the gap.

Since it is not altogether certain that you sit down with a perfect posture at the first try, you should do the sitting exercise after the above exercises. They have surely improved your standing posture, which is the one you should bring with you when you sit down.

1   Stand with your feet at shoulder distance, and with your arms along the sides of your body. Relax.

2   Sit down on your shinbones, with the knees quite far apart, and your buttocks resting on your heels, which are leaning slightly outward. Your big toes touch lightly. Put the palms of your hands on your thighs, so that the fingers point in an angle forward-inward, but keep your elbows quite close to the sides of your body. Your hips, your upper body, your neck and head, should all have *the same posture as when standing up.* Check if that is the case. Do not correct your position in any way. That would only make your body get lost in it. Just feel it. If your position is not so good, trust that it will be better next time.

3   Lift your upper body right up, without changing its angle or posture. Lower it again – rather quickly, almost

氣

like falling – just by relaxing your leg muscles. Check if your posture or the angle of your upper body has changed. It should not. This corresponds to the balance exercise above, where you go up on your toes. You can repeat this once or twice, but not really more than that.

4   Slide your knees toward one another, until the distance between them is about the width of a fist. You can put your fist between them, to use as measurement. Narrowing the angle of your legs like this straightens your posture, and gives you an improved stature, making you feel proud and refreshed.

5   Stand up and assume the position

氣

you started with. Check if your body posture has changed. It should not.

6   Make the whole exercise again. Once is never, and so on.

This exercise gets you acquainted with how your body really wants to sit – at least your upper body. Your knees and ankles may have some objections. Therefore it is important to do this exercise with some regularity – all your life. High age should not be an insurmountable obstacle, if you just previously have some experience with this kind of sitting.

Everyday life tends to be full of unsuitable sitting in bad chairs, so this exercise is a healthy alternative. You do not need to do this exercise as much as you spend time in chairs, far from it. But if you never sit in any other way than in chairs, then all that sitting is sure to sabotage any work you do on your posture. With some frequency, allow your body to experience what sitting with a good posture is like.

Meditate
While we are seated with special attention to the posture, we would be negligent if we did not make some comments about meditation – not exactly its purpose, but the position one should have to do it best. There is a lot to think about.

In Eastern meditation your body posture should be the same as in the above exercises. You should have a proud stature that is still relaxed, where your body has sort of fallen into place, so that you are in balance.

Usually, seated meditation is done in positions where you have your legs in front of you, instead of under your body. Not that the former position is superior, but because it is more comfortable for the legs, at length – and those who meditate regularly, often do it for quite some time. But such positions cause problems for the back. It is difficult to stop the hips from tilting backward, which causes the back to bend. This is often countered by sitting on a pillow. That

氣

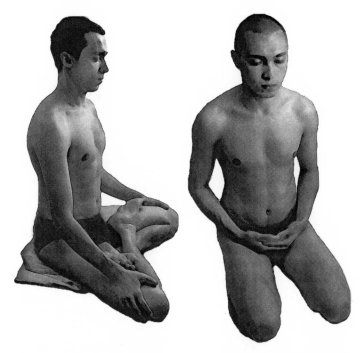

gives a better angle between your back and your legs. It is not regarded as cheating.

Below, I still focus on the kind of sitting where you have your legs under your body – the Japanese way. You do not need to do the same. What sitting position you choose is of little importance, since the details I go through below have nothing to do with the position of your legs. Sit as you please, but try to follow the other advice I give.

1   Your head should have an angle where the fontanel, the spot where the parts of your skull closed when you were an infant, is the highest point. Thereby, your chin is slightly closer to the chest than normal. But you should not consciously press your chin down, because that causes unnatural tension. It is better to think that the neck and the back of your head are extended

氣

upward, as if somebody grabbed the hair by your fontanel and pulled. You can actually do that, yourself. Pinch some of the hair at your fontanel, and pull upward. That way, your head gets the right angle. It is also the right angle for all the previous exercises.

2   Your eyes should almost be closed, with just a thin opening, and you should look with indifference at a point on the floor, about four to six feet in front of you. In my opinion, closed eyes are also fine, as long as you do not allow your eyes to roll up. When the eyes turn upward, your mind is tempted to go to sleep. Your lips should be closed, but your jaws not. Keep a small gap between the teeth of the upper and lower jaws. The tip of your tongue should lightly touch the roof of your mouth.

3   Your hands should meet in a closed figure that rests on your lap, touching or almost touching your belly. What figure the hands form is of minor importance, as long as it is sort of closed and you keep it fixed. It helps you to stay awake, but also to remain within yourself. A classic position of the hands is where the tips of the thumbs meet, and one hand rests on the palm of the other. Whether the right or left hand should be the inner one is a matter of much discussion, also traditionally. You just choose what feels best at length. The thumbs should be extended, as should the other fingers.

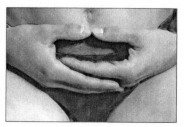

氣

But remember that you can choose any hand figure. Experiment with it, and trust your own judgment.

4   Breathe with your belly – more about that later – and relax as much as you can in this position. Let ambitions and all kinds of thoughts pour away from your brain. In meditation you should *think about nothing* (at least in Zen). That is not easy. Thoughts inevitably appear, and there is no point in trying to stop them. What you can do is to accept them, and at the same time conclude that they are not important right now. So you let them slide away, one after the other. By time, your brain will become rather empty. Well, it can take years of practice. Thoughts are gradually dissolved if you neither make them important, nor try desperately to hold them off.

5   Sit as long as you can without discomfort. When you get uncomfortable, your mind gets distracted, so prolonging the meditation is of little use. Still, by practice you can increase the time you are able to sit with ease. Not that it is important to sit for very long, really. The one who is determined to sit for a long time might not be enough focused on the meditation. In that case, it is better with short periods, done from beginning to end with a dedicated spirit. Settle for a few min-

氣

utes at first, and increase only if you feel that you benefit from it.

6 When you are properly seated for meditation, breathe with your belly, and let your thoughts dissolve. Then you will increasingly be situated right in the middle of your center – something that we will also return to, below. It is not exactly an exercise where qi shall flow in abundance, but all the body channels shall be open, so that no tension appears. Although meditation is not at all a way to repose, it becomes quite restful and thereby liberating to the mind as well as the body. You can feel complications lose their grip, inner knots get untied, and trouble ease.

Even though meditation is beneficial in so many ways, you should not meditate in order to achieve certain specific goals. Again, this is particularly true about Zen. Instead, the purpose is to let go of ambition and strife. You sit to sit. Neither to reach satori, that sudden moment of clarity, nor to feel good – although that would not hurt.

The core of meditation is such that you cannot get hold of it, if you aim for something particular at the outset – even if that aim is to get in touch with the core. It is elusive. Actually, its very nature is such that it cannot exist where there is purpose. You do not feel any scent if you hold your breath, and the core of meditation is not revealed to you if you search for it. This purposeless attitude is particularly difficult for westerners to adapt.

As I have said, meditation is slightly outside the theme of this book, but not more so than that you can meditate now and then, in connection to the other exercises. If so, do it only for equally short times. Do not sit any longer than you have the urge to do, or are able without discomfort. And do not meditate with higher frequency than you do the other exercises. More than once a day would be overdoing it, at least in this perspective.

If you are attracted to meditation, I recommend that

氣

Meditating Buddha.

you use the exercises in this book to foster your mind and body into the best possible condition for meditation. Only when you are pleased with the result should you move on to spend significant time on meditating. At that moment, you are probably ready to quit doing the exercises of this book regularly.

氣

Relaxation

Relax. That sounds easy enough, but in reality it is an almost superhuman task to do properly. Certainly, it is possible to make some muscles rest, without too much complication. You can do it as simply as sitting down in a chair, or lie down on a bed. That way, anyone can immediately relax to a certain degree. But there are so many muscles in the body. Even when you lie in your bed, lots of them are more or less tense.

Some muscles have important tasks around the clock, so they are never allowed to rest. But many others are tense, causing nothing but their slow deterioration. Some of these muscles have been unnecessarily tense for so long that you do not notice it anymore. That does not mean their tension lacks influence. They inhibit the natural flows in your body, and wear themselves down. The really difficult task is to make also these muscles relax.

Relaxation is not an absolute concept with just one obvious meaning. It is relative. You can be more or less relaxed, but probably never completely relaxed – while you are alive. What you need to do is to find the level of relaxation that suits you, and makes your body comfortable.

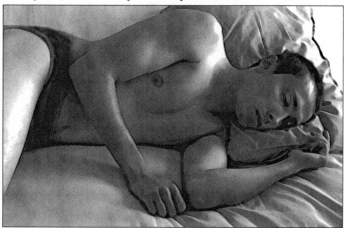

氣

For a good flow of qi, it is not necessary that the muscles in your body become like jelly. The important thing is that they do not stiffen to the extent that they restrain the flow. One could say that the muscles need to be in a natural state. Whether they rest or contract, this should be in accordance with the bodily functions and the activity you are involved in. They should do what is needed of them – neither more nor less.

When we do something strenuous, we often struggle not only with the muscles needed for the task, but also with muscles that contribute nothing. For example, when making an effort with something, we tend to tighten our jaws or pull up our shoulders, often as an unconscious reflex because of the mental strain. Such superfluous behavior needs to be worked off, if you want to intensify your qi flow and avoid overstrain, the tear that otherwise increases through the years.

On the other hand, if you are involved in something that demands powerful work with some of your muscles, the qi flow is stimulated when these muscles get active. They do not need to relax in order for qi to flow freely through them, and through the rest of the body.

So, the relaxation that this book aims at is one where the muscles work in a harmonious and functional way. Certainly, this also means that when they have nothing to do, they should really rest and be soft as jelly.

This natural functionality of the muscles reveals a pursuable path for learning to relax them – the contrast between work and rest. Although it is difficult to feel what muscles contract unnecessarily, you can make the difference apparent by switching between contracting and releasing them. That is mainly how the relaxation exercises below work.

Actually, the best method to relax is by breathing. Most breathing exercises have the effect that they help the body toward increased relaxation. But it is difficult to teach a body that is too tense how to breathe properly. A somewhat relaxed body, on the other hand, gets more and more relaxed

Zen monk in a tree, by Shohaku Soga (1730-1781).

氣

by itself, from breathing exercises. Therefore the order in this book is such that we begin with some relaxation exercises, and work on breathing after that.

When you have learned the exercises of this book, you will surely mix the order of them, and let them blend so that posture, relaxation, breathing, and so forth, are all trained in each of them. That is quite correct. The different aspects are connected, so they need to be practiced jointly – like it takes several people in cooperation to erect a huge statue.

Now, on to the relaxation exercises. The first ones are some concrete exercises in changing between the contraction and release of muscles, so that you become aware of the difference and thereby easier make muscles relax when they should. It is quite difficult to relax muscles that are tense even when they do not need to be, because their tension has become an unconscious habit. So, do these exercises primarily to explore the difference between tension and relaxation, and how to consciously switch from the one to the other.

I recommend you to follow the order given below, at least in the beginning, when you familiarize yourself with the exercises and what they do to you.

Clench and open

Here you focus on the hands. They are almost constantly at work, so it can be difficult to relax them enough to be pleasantly soft and supple. When the hands are active, not only all the muscles from the wrist out to the fingertips are used, but also a number of muscles along the arms, up to the shoulders – sometimes also muscles on the back. But you do not have to think about that. Concentrate on your hands, and the rest will take care of itself.

1   You can make this exercise standing or sitting, but it does not work as well if you are lying down. You should close your eyes, to feel more clearly what happens in your muscles, and not to be distracted by the surroundings.

氣

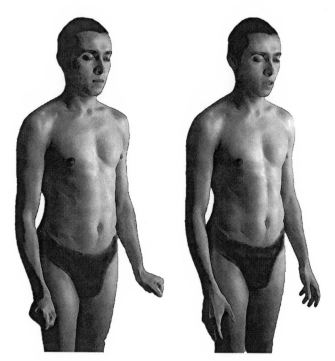

2　With your arms along the sides of your body, clench your fists as hard as you can, at the same time as you *inhale through your nose*. Also the muscles of your arms and shoulders will contract, which is good.

3　Open your hands suddenly and relax them, at the same time as you *exhale through your mouth*.

4　Do it again. Once is never... You can continue as long as you notice a difference in how your hands, arms, and shoulders feel when they relax.

When the hands feel really soft and supple, and the arms hang down lazily, you are well on your way. This actually helps many other parts of the body to relax, since the hands are involved in most things you do. When they rest, a substantial portion of the body does the same.

氣

Shoulders up and down

The shoulders are often the real villains in a bad posture, and the consequences of it. A bad posture does in itself cause tense shoulders, and the other way around, but there are many things that can create unnecessary tension in the shoulders. The following exercise is a way of countering the tension that shoulders can have, even if they are straight and the posture is good.

1   You can make this exercise standing up as well as sitting, but not lying down. I recommend that you close your eyes.

2   With your arms along the sides of your body, pull your shoulders as high up as you can, so that they almost touch the ears. Do it at the same time as you *inhale through your nose.* Your arms should still hang loosely, and your hands should be open and inactive.

3   Let your shoulders suddenly fall down at the same time as you *exhale through your mouth.*

4   Repeat. You can continue with this exercise as long as you feel that it makes the shoulders relax more.

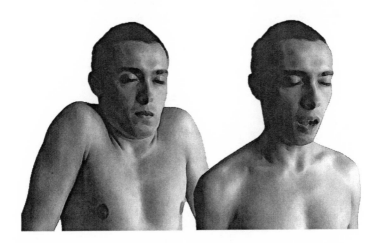

氣

Note that this should be done after the exercise with the hands clenching and opening. If they are done in the reverse order, there is a risk that the exercise with the hands counters the result of the shoulder exercise.

Grimace

The face has almost innumerable muscles, and they certainly do not get to rest that often. I have heard somewhere that the most muscles relax when we smile, but I doubt it – maybe if it is of Mona-Lisa's mysterious kind. I bet that most muscles relax when we have a blank expression in our faces. That is not so easy to accomplish at will as it would seem. You can work your way toward it with this exercise and the next one. So, both these exercises should be done one after the other – or at the same time – and with the purpose of getting a blank expression in your face, one without any particular mood or sentiment.

1   You can do this exercise standing or sitting. It is possible to do it lying down as well, but that is not recommendable.

2   Grimace with all your face. Tighten every muscle as if you took a bite on a lemon. Your whole face should wrinkle. At the same time, *inhale through your nose.*

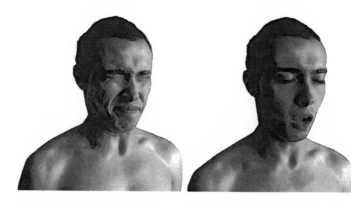

氣

3   Relax your face suddenly, and open the mouth by letting your chin fall. At the same time, *exhale through your mouth.*

4   Repeat at least once. There is no point in doing it that many times. Actually, it is not easy to do it equally well if repeated more than two or three times.

In addition to being kind of comical, this exercise actually helps to relax your facial muscles. You may be able to feel how the pressure in them sort of releases from inside, as if they softened and got a little heavier. Don't worry that it will make your facial features flabby – on the contrary, it will make them more springy and energetic.

Empty gaze

Of course there is some minute muscle work going on inside the eyes, but this exercise is for the face muscles around the eyes. Also, it is to help create the blank facial expression mentioned above. Since the eyes are essential in any facial expression, an empty gaze is needed to make that blank face. Remember that this exercise can be done immediately after the previous one, or at the same time.

1   You can do this exercise standing, sitting, or lying down. It is good if you have a clear view in front of you, at least some ten feet ahead – but the more the better. If you are indoors, you can look out a window.

2   Close your eyes very firmly. Squeeze the eyelids shut, so that most of your face wrinkles, at the same time as you *inhale through the nose.*

3   Open the eyes, suddenly and completely, at the same time as you *exhale through your mouth.* You will notice that it takes a little while before your eyes have focused on what you have in front of you, and during that short time your gaze is quite empty. You want to prolong that moment, so *try not to focus your gaze* on anything at all.

氣

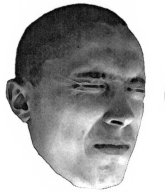

It can be hard at first, but by practice you should be able to extend the period before your eyes fix on something.

4   Repeat, preferably several times – especially if you find it hard to keep the empty gaze more than a couple of seconds. If you do not improve at it, then stop with the exercise. You can return to it another time. It is likely to get better each time you try it anew.

The empty gaze is not only restful, but also linked to a state of mind that is particularly delightful and rewarding – similar to the one you can reach in meditation. Empty mind is how Zen describes it. You can really relax if you can have an empty mind between the times when you involve yourself in something or other.

Huddle up
In this exercise there are probably not that many muscles shifting from contraction to release, at least not in an obvious way. Now the body as a whole is the target. You are to feel the difference between the contracted and compact on one side, and the opened and extended on the other – in your whole body. Thereby, you express in the whole what the parts should learn. Your body shows what its muscles should do. But do not think much about it. Just do the exercise and let it work its way.

氣

1   Here you should sit on the floor. You can sit on a blanket or carpet, but not something as thick as a mattress. It is good if you close your eyes, so that you are more sensitive to what happens inside of you.

2   Sit in a squatting position, with your buttocks and the soles of your feet on the floor. Embrace your bent legs and press them to your chest. Also, bend your neck so that your head leans forward. This you should do while you *inhale through your nose*.

3   Release the legs and stretch out your body slowly, until you lie flat on your back on the floor. At the same time, *exhale through your mouth*. Be careful, so that you do not hit the back of your head on the floor, or experience some other discomfort. But try to reach the final position before your exhalation ends.

4   Remain in this position for a little while, and feel it. It should be very relaxed and you should feel open.

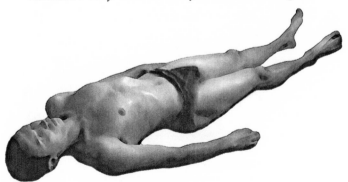

氣

5   Repeat. Once is never. You can continue as long as you feel that it gets increasingly pleasant to lie down. When you notice no difference, you might as well stop.

You can certainly do this exercise in connection to those regarding posture. Well, you can mix it in with just about any exercise, if you like. Apart from teaching your body to relax, it works on your attitude, because the body and the mind affect one another. The difference between the crouching and the extended position has an exact mental counterpart, which is actually stimulated by the physical exercise. As your body feels increasingly open, so does your mind.

Hang

Unfortunately, for this exercise you need a tool. That says something about how rarely we assume this position. You simply need something to hang from. Outside of the gym hall of a school, that is not so easy to find. If you do not find anything suitable, you might be unable to do this exercise. Don't worry about it. It is not essential. Try it once or twice, when you have the opportunity, and that is fine.

Even if you have the means of repeating it as often as you like, you really need not do it frequently – unless you notice that it does a lot of good for you.

1   Initially you are standing up, of course. It is good if you have few and loose clothes. Especially, you should not have anything tight around your waist, hips, or legs.

2   Grab the tool you have found to hang from, and heave yourself up until your

氣

feet leave the floor – without you having to bend your legs.

3   Hang for a little while and breathe calmly. You can also swing your legs around a little, and wag your hips. Feel how free they are, when they do not need to work on holding up your body. When you hang like this, your hips can actually be more relaxed than when you lie down on the floor.

4   Stop when it gets too straining for your arms. Take a short break and repeat, if you have the strength. You can continue as long as your legs and hips enjoy it, and the muscles of your arms don't protest too much.

In many ways, the hips are the power center for your whole body, and the legs carry the whole load. They deserve a break. This exercise also helps you feel their condition. If your hips are unevenly strained, you should feel it when you hang there. And when your legs hang freely you will mainly notice in what shape your knees are.

As you stand on the floor again, you should try to avoid a straining body posture. It should be easy enough, with the help of what you learned about your body when hanging there.

Rest heavily

As stated earlier, it is not easy to relax fully, even when lying down. We do not even relax when we sleep, not completely. Nor is sleep an even and steady state of mind all through the night. There are periods of higher and lower activity for the brain, as well as for the body. No wonder that relaxation is so hard to accomplish.

Sleep is a bit devious. Although it is our primary method of rest, there are many situations when it is not the most successful at it. When you are strained or under pressure, it can be difficult to fall asleep, or to sleep long and deep enough to recuperate. If you have no other method at your disposal, you are caught in a trap that might by time become a vicious spiral.

But sleep has no exclusive right to rest – far from it. It has other functions as well, about which we only know parts. Therefore it does not always make the priorities we might wish for. If you want to rest, it is important to focus on this task, even if it means setting sleep aside for a while. To accomplish a really effective rest you need to be awake – wide-awake.

In the following exercise it is not exactly qi that has the main role. This is more of a process that can be compared to hypnosis, or in any case self-suggestion. Still, the method is closely related to the qi exercises that follow later on in this book: You have to take control of yourself with the powers of thought, will, and fantasy. Thereby it is an excellent exercise of these powers.

1   Lie down on the floor, flat on your back. Not on a bed, where you are likely to doze off, on the other hand not so uncomfortably that your concentration is disturbed. Lie on a blanket or a carpet, and you should be fine. Keep your arms along the sides of your body, and your feet at shoulder distance. Wear as few and loose clothes as possible. Close your eyes.

2   Take a few deep breaths. When you are familiar with correct breathing, which is presented later on in this book, you should use such breathing. Keep a slow beat,

氣

where you allow a few seconds of stillness between inhalations and exhalations. In particular, extend your exhalations and wait a little before inhaling again.

3   In your mind, focus on how heavily your body rests on the floor, and feel this heaviness increase by time. *Accept and enjoy gravity.* That universal force keeps you down, without you having to do anything at all. Let your body experience this.

4   The contrast between fighting and accepting gravity is evident if you lift one of your hands from the floor. It takes an effort, although a small one. Then let it fall back to the floor, and the strain of keeping it up is gone. Do not lift it very high at all, because then you will be reluctant to let it fall freely to the floor. Your muscles slow the fall down in order to protect the hand, whether you are conscious of it or not. The hand should fall without any interference, simply by giving in to gravity. Five to ten inches are enough.

5   You can repeat this lifting and letting go of your hand. You can also do it with a foot, or with the feet and hands at once. The important thing is that you notice the contrast between tension and relaxation, like in the previous exercises. You should also be increasingly aware of how gravity presses you to the floor. When you feel this very clearly, just lie still and accept it.

6   The more you accept gravity, the more you feel how heavy your body is. Do not reject this feeling, but encourage it as much as you can. By each breath, especially in the exhalations, you should feel *heavier and*

氣

heavier. Lightness is for the body connected to movement, whereas the feeling of heaviness is connected to rest. The heavier you feel, the more your body rests.

7   This self-suggestion can be enhanced if you imagine to be sinking deeper, as if through the floor, because of your increasing heaviness and your acceptance of gravity. Then there is a risk that you doze off. Try it anyway. It does not hurt to fall asleep in this way. It increases the chance of particularly restful sleep. It will probably not be that long, but can prove to be quite invigorating.

The most important lesson in this exercise is that you relate to both rest and sleep with an active mind.

Passively awaiting a restful state of mind and body is usually insufficient. Sometimes you cannot even fall asleep by simply lying in your bed and waiting for it. Then some initiative of yours is needed. You have to actively get involved in this or another exercise, to change your state of mind.

When you train your mind for it, rest is much easier – also in stressful situations. Even if you do not fall asleep, the time you spend on this kind of training is advantageous. And that confidence will make you fall asleep more easily.

氣

Breathing

Now we are closing in on the essence of exercising qi and its flow. Breathing is sort of a sibling to qi. That is how close they are – almost like twins, but not identical ones. The air that flows through our lungs at each breath has got many similarities to the qi flow, but is still essentially different. That goes for oxygen as well, the substance that breathing transports to the blood, and the blood distributes to all of the body – just like qi. Still, they are different.

Anyway, their similarities are enough for correct and concentrated breathing exercises to be the most effective way of getting your qi flow going. So, now it is time for exercises working on your breathing to make it even more similar to the qi flow. If we devote ourselves wholeheartedly to one of the twins, the other cannot stay away for long.

Good breathing is a blessing in life, surpassed by few things. It gives a sense of delight, and is so stimulating that it must be compared to inspiration. That is indicated by the very word inspire, *inspirare* in Latin, which originally means breathing – more precisely breathing in. That says a lot. Breathing can inspire, especially breathing in. Take a deep breath and feel your soul soar.

When you inhale you receive, and when you exhale you give. That is the rhythm of life. The one is impossible without the other. They are opposites that are forever linked, similar to the pair of *yin* and *yang* in classical Chinese cosmology.

At first, inhalation and exhalation need to be treated as two evident opposites, but by time they should sort of blend, so that the change between them becomes less and less perceivable. Breathing shall become a constant life-giving flow through the body, a concrete mirroring of the hidden ether that is qi.

When exploring breathing and its nature, we start by making a clear distinction between in and out.

氣

The Taoist immortal Lu Tung-Pin, by Sesson Shukei (c. 1504-1589).

氣

Extend your exhalation

Of course, there must be an absolute balance between inhalation and exhalation. Otherwise breathing just would not work. Still, lots of people are most concerned about the former. We tend to focus on breathing in, to the extent that we completely neglect what happens when we breathe out – as if it were not that important. This discrepancy needs to be corrected, in order to create a flowing breath.

One effect of giving priority to inhalation is that the lungs are almost completely filled with air all the time, as if they did not want to give it away. Therefore, breathing is only done on that marginal lung volume remaining. In that case, you are forced to breathe quickly in order to get enough fresh air. That rushes and stresses the body and mind. It also easily causes you to get almost painfully out of breath, so that you have trouble even with modest hardships.

Only by emptying yourself of air can you fill yourself with it, and that is the only way of assuring that you get plenty of fresh air into your lungs. So, the first exercise is simply to breathe out properly, in order to fill the lungs anew – deeply.

1   You can stand, sit, or lie down, just what you like. It does not matter. But try to have the good posture that you have learned from previous exercises, and avoid any clothing that sits tight on your body. Wear loose clothes, and as few as possible.

2   Inhale normally, through your nose.

3   Exhale through your mouth – as much as you can, without losing your good posture. Continue the exhalation as long as possible – *and then some.*

4   Close your mouth and *let the inhalation happen automatically.* Do not let your conscious mind control your inhalation. You will observe that you breathe in as suddenly as if the air was pushed down your lungs, like a vacuum suddenly opening to the outside world. This way, the inhaled air feels particularly fresh and refreshing.

氣

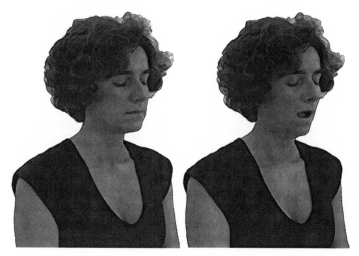

5   When this sudden rush of air has entered your lungs, you should not consciously continue with the inhalation. Instead, you open your mouth and breathe out, at least as much as last time.

6   Repeat as long as it feels good. Remember to keep your good posture. If you get dizzy by the increased oxygen intake this kind of breathing causes, slow down by prolonging your exhalations. You can also take short pauses between inhalation and exhalation, but do not try to change the speed of the former.

You can do this exercise as much as you like. It is particularly useful when you feel tired or just a bit inert.

This is also the way to catch your breath after an ordeal. When we get out of breath, we are so eager to get fresh air that we forget to exhale the old air. That makes it hard to ever get enough air. So, when you are out jogging or doing something else that makes you out of breath, try to concentrate on the exhalations. You will quickly get more stamina than usual. Strive to push the old air out of your lungs. You do not have to worry about the inhalations, because they take care of themselves.

氣

This kind of inhaling – suddenly and automatically, after a long exhalation – is invigorating. You will find it quite inspiring. When you face some task that demands the most of your abilities, this breathing is excellent preparation. It gives you lust, power, and the kind of spiritual inebriation that is the true mother of invention.

Lower your breath
Extending the breath, like in the above exercise, also makes it deeper – but not to the extent that this exercise is able.

A breath that is to stimulate the qi flow must take place deep in your body, what is usually called belly breathing or diaphragm breathing. Most people breathe exclusively with their chest, maybe as high up as the shoulders. This leads to short breaths and persistent tension around the shoulders. Such breathing also afflicts the mind with unrest and insecurity. That is as far from relaxation as one can get.

The Eastern ideal is instead to breathe with the belly, actually as low as the bottom of the abdomen. Of course it is still the lungs that get the air, but you should feel very clearly that the shoulders relax while your abdomen moves with the breaths you take, as if the air goes all the way down there. Opera singers do the same kind of breathing. It carries their voices better, and gives them power to really sing out.

If you have never tried belly breathing, it can be quite tricky to learn. Breathing is something the body does without the conscious mind being involved in it – around the clock, and year after year. Such habits are difficult to change. We continue with the same old habits, if we do not make the proper efforts to alter them. Your body has to learn a new way of doing what it has done in pretty much the same way all your life. Expect it to take time, maybe years, before you are belly breathing without having to think about it. No doubt, you have to practice it daily.

First you must find that deep breathing, in the lower abdomen. This is the most effective method I know, to accomplish that. Still, count on quite some time before you get it right.

氣

1   You can stand or sit in this exercise, but the best is prob-
    ably if you lie down on your back, like in some of the
    previous exercises. When you have learned to find a
    deep belly breathing, it is not necessary anymore to do
    it lying down. By then you should be able to do it sit-
    ting, standing, or even walking. Loose clothing is help-
    ful, and in the beginning probably quite necessary.
    Loosen what might be tight, especially around your
    belly. The less clothes the better. Even very loose gar-
    ments have a tendency to slightly inhibit your breath-
    ing.

2   Relax and take a few normal breaths, so that you calm
    down.

3   Put the palm of one of your hands on your belly, be-
    tween the navel and the crotch. There should be good
    contact, but do not press the hand on your belly. Ob-
    serve that it is the palm of your hand that is important,
    and not the fingers. They should be passive. Otherwise
    they can confuse and disturb your breathing.

4   Breathe in and then start a slow exhalation. Do not
    breathe out through your mouth, which tends to bring
    the breathing up toward your chest, but through your
    nose.

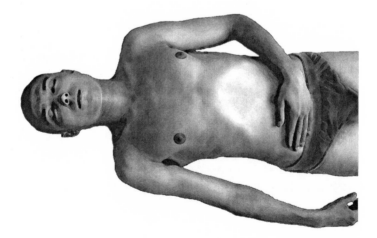

氣

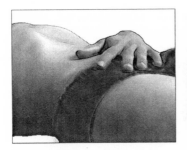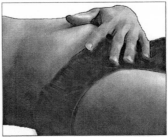

5   Now, make a sudden and forceful exhalation, by which you try to push the hand on your belly. Make it bump, *only by your sudden exhalation.* Do not push with your body. The hips should not move at all. The push should come from within your stomach. In the beginning it is probably a kind of wave from your chest and downward, but by time you should be able to do the push with your stomach, and nothing else. It is tricky at first. Try again and again, until you succeed.

6   Take a new breath and repeat the pushing of your hand with your exhalation. Remember to *start the exhalation slowly, before you make the push.* Otherwise the body tends to resist and get tense. You should repeat the exercise until you feel that you manage to push the palm of your hand from inside your stomach, without the rest of the body helping noticeably.

This exercise is intended to lower the breathing of a person who is not used to breathe with the belly. When you have learned this, it is no longer necessary to repeat the exercise. Later on, you may benefit from testing it now and then, although you know how to belly breathe, just to check that you really breathe as far down in your abdomen as you wish.

Do not underestimate the depth of proper belly breathing. If you succeed when you hold your hand in the middle between the navel and your crotch, continue by moving it further down, closer to your crotch, and try again. If you can breathe down at the very bottom of your abdomen, then you have opened your breathing completely.

It is advantageous, not to say necessary, to let this exercise be followed by the next one – especially if you are in the process of learning belly breathing, and trying to make it a habit.

Belly breathing

The above exercise is an effective way of bringing down your breathing to the belly. Then you have to learn to breathe that way normally, making belly breathing something that comes naturally to you. That is what this exercise is for, so try to do it right after the previous one.

When you feel that you have no problem getting the breathing down to your lower abdomen, you can skip the above exercise and go directly to this one. Actually, they do not differ that much.

1   You can walk, stand, or sit down, but in the beginning the easiest is to lie on your back. Your clothes should be loose, especially on the belly, and the less clothes you have on, the better.

2   Put the palm of one of your hands on your belly, about midway between your navel and your crotch – or closer to the crotch if you can get your breathing that low. Remember to keep a good contact between your palm and belly, without pushing.

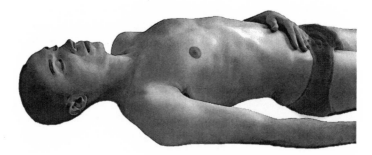

3   Start a slow and deep inhalation through your nose, and try to do it in such a way that your belly pushes on the hand. This means that the belly expands when you breathe in.

4   Continue with a long exhalation through your mouth – and this time, too, there should be a pressure from your belly onto your hand. That may seem odd, but *both when you inhale and when you exhale the belly should expand*, pressing on your hand. Thereby, the belly seems to be constantly growing, which is fine. Do not worry about your figure, since this is just how it feels.

5   Go on with this breathing, your belly pressing on your hand. When you feel that you do it right without any particular effort, you can take away the hand – but continue with the same breathing for a while.

6   If your breathing tends to move up toward your chest, and you notice that the chest starts moving at each breath, then put your hand back on the belly, and try again.

7   Continue to breathe this way as long as you want. Take your time – it is supposed to become a new habit of yours. If you notice that you get very tense when trying to belly breathe, you should not do it for more than a few minutes. Instead, repeat the exercise at another time.

Of course, the hand is on your belly to help you learn deep breathing, and to make you feel clearly when you do it right. But the hand is not only a passive tool for measuring the effects of your exercise. It is active, and sort of calls on your breathing. A kind of dialogue appears between the hand and your belly, an exchange that helps you along. It would not work nearly as well if you tried putting a dead object on your belly. A live one other than your hand, though, would work at least as well. You can try with the friendly hand of a loved one, or a cat curled up on your belly, peacefully purring. Cats know everything about qi.

氣

A good way of testing your breathing is to put one hand on your belly, and the other on your chest. Then you will notice to what extent you breathe with your chest or your belly – under what hand there is the most activity. The best is if just about nothing happens under the hand on your chest, and lots under the hand on your belly. That might take a while.

Do not start with this two-hands test when you try to learn belly breathing. Both hands might call on your breathing, so you will end up with breaths that are evenly divided between the belly and the chest. You want all the breathing in your belly, so wait with this test until you are well on your way.

Count on needing to do this belly breathing exercise quite a lot, in order to establish this new breathing habit. I doubt that it can be done in a shorter time than a year, no matter how much you do it daily. You will learn to belly breathe quite quickly, but it will take time before that breathing becomes an automatic habit. It may even take significantly longer than a year, but you should notice that each time you do the exercise it comes easier and more freely. It gets increasingly natural to you. And your body will be delighted, because this is how it wants to breathe.

氣

Every infant knows this. Just watch them breathe.

When you start to get the hang of it, you can exercise belly breathing in any position, whenever and wherever. You can do it on your work place, behind the wheels of your car, when you ride a bicycle, or when you run. Do it at any given opportunity during your everyday life, so that you really confirm to your body that this should be your new habit.

The hand on your belly is a good help when you introduce yourself to belly breathing, but when you have gotten familiar with it, you will find that the hand is not necessary anymore. You just need to tell yourself to belly breathe, and you will. Then it is starting to become automatic. You just remind yourself, and you start belly breathing immediately – and it goes on, without you having to pay any attention to it.

By time, you only need to remind yourself now and then, when for some reason your breathing jumped up to your chest, or maybe it just lost some of its grandeur. Then you only have to make one conscious deep breath to get it going again.

Your breathing will become your foremost internal resource of power, confidence, and vitality. Whenever you need it, get it going by taking a big and deep breath. When you have established belly breathing as a habit, you just need to remind yourself of the fact that you actually do breathe correctly, in order to get on top of things – no matter how stressful or straining they are.

Breathe in a square

Breathing has more to give – a lot more. When you have a good belly breathing going, it has a power and a depth that are vitalizing and cleansing, reminding of its closeness to qi.

Breathing can be an even more direct help to awake and increase your qi flow. The following breathing exercise has this purpose. *Now it is time to breathe qi.*

How that works is explained in the exercise description, but do not focus solely on this aspect. Do it like a pure

氣 Qi 81

breathing exercise. Otherwise there is a risk that your conscious mind takes over and brushes the bodily experience aside. That will not help your qi flow. So, settle for what a pleasant and calming way of breathing it is. Then qi can flow freely through your body, instead of being hindered by your conscious ambition to steer it.

1   For this exercise you should assume a relaxed and peaceful position. Therefore you should avoid standing up, which would demand of you to keep your balance. That can cause some tension and disturbance. So, sit down with a good posture, or lie on your back. Loose clothing is fine, but not as important as with most of the previous exercises.

2   Breathe normally through your nose for a while, so that you slow down and relax. Belly breathing is great, but actually not necessary. Already before you have learned a good belly breathing, you can get a lot from this exercise. But of course, the deeper you breathe, the more you get.

3   Now, start a strictly regulated breathing: choose *a fixed time for each phase* of it. Do not make it too long. Later on, you will notice why. Settle for something like five seconds. That means you should make an inhalation, which lasts for five seconds, followed by a just as long exhalation. You do not have to time it with a clock. It needs not be that exact. It is enough that you count slowly to five. Do it silently, or it will interfere with your breathing.

4   When this works smoothly, you should add the same length of time after the inhalation, where you hold your breath with *a feeling of continued inhalation.* Do not tighten your body to hold your breath, but sort of continue with the inhalation although you get no more air.

5   After exhaling for the same length of time, add an equal period where you have *a feeling of continued exhalation,* although no more air leaves you. You will notice that it

氣

is harder to extend the period after an exhalation. The body is eager to get new air. That is why you should not choose a longer period of time than you manage comfortably.

6   Now you are breathing in a square: Five seconds of inhaling, five seconds of a continued feeling of inhaling, five seconds of exhaling, and five seconds of a continued feeling of exhaling. Do it over and over. You can keep it up as long as you like, but only if you are able to feel like breathing in or out at the intervals when you actually hold your breath.

7   *That feeling of inhaling and exhaling is qi.* It is not more odd than that. When you feel that you inhale something, or exhale something, and it is not air – then it is qi. The more clear this sense of breathing without air is to you, the stronger your qi flows.

Yes, it is qi you sort of breathe, when there is no air flowing. You also breathe qi when air passes in or out, but then it is not as easy to distinguish.

This exercise is an excellent way of getting familiar with qi and its nature, how qi feels and works. You will probably notice that the breathing without air is just as invigorating as regular breathing, although in a different way. The best way to describe it is that you breathe pure inspiration – or intention.

氣

But whatever words we choose for it, they are bland when compared to the actual experience. So when you do the exercise, concentrate on the experience and do not bother to interpret it intellectually. That would only disturb it.

Of course, when you get more used to this exercise, you can skip the step where you breathe air only, in two phases. Go directly to the square, with four phases of breathing.

You should also practice your ability to recognize your qi breathing when you breathe normally. It is there, as well. That should be increasingly obvious to you. Also when you are breathing in a square, you do good to focus on your qi breathing in all the four phases.

The differences between breathing air and no air should dissolve by time, and lose their significance. The essence of your breathing should be its qi flow, and you can feel it all through.

It is also good to extend the length of time you choose, when you get better at this. You should never make the time so long that you feel frustrated during the fourth phase, before breathing in anew. That phase is the most difficult to extend, so it should be decisive when you choose the length of the intervals you try. It is not a competition of any kind, so you need only to find a time that is optimal for your experience of the exercise.

氣

Extension

With the correct posture, relaxation, and deep breathing, you can easily get your qi flowing and be increasingly aware of it. As you progress, it gets more and more important that qi flows through your body – and out of it.

Here too, the similarity to breathing is evident. You cannot keep the air inside. It has to get out for new air to enter. It is the same with qi. It has to exit the body in order for new qi to enter.

In the East, qi that is held inside is described as getting old and bad, sort of stale. Although an inner flow of qi is invigorating and healing, if qi is kept inside it becomes almost hazardous to the health. You feel worse, your body gets weaker, and your ailments increase. If you work up a powerful flow of qi inside of you, but do not let it out, then it becomes frustrating. You get nervous, impatient, and increasingly tense, not unlike any closed container filled to the point of breaking.

Qi should flow out through the body, and not stay inside of it.

The exercise of breathing in a square, above, indicates the same. The air you breathe does not stay in the body, but leaves when it has been used. The qi you awaken inside of you should be used and dispatched. Then new qi enters your body, whether you do a breathing exercise or not.

Really, you always use your qi, whatever you do. That is the nature of the life spirit. But when you stimulate the qi flow and make it grow, there may be an imbalance between in and out. So, you have to stimulate the outward flow of qi to the extent you stimulate the qi emergence inside of you. You have to spend what you gain.

The following exercises, dealing with the extension of qi, have that function. But they also show, in a general way, how you can utilize your qi. This is necessary in order to keep you well-being in the long run. Probably, you want to explore the use of qi anyway, out of curiosity. You should.

氣

You will discover that most things in life become different when you consciously use qi and get increasingly accustomed to it. Different and still the same. What changes is the feeling, the experience.

You will probably notice this, already when you try out the following exercises for the first time.

These exercises should not be done lying down, mainly because that is quite a passive position. Now it is time for you to become active, and to apply the abilities you have gained from previous exercises. So, the best is to sit or stand – maybe even walk about, when that fits the specific exercise.

Your basic attitude in these exercises should be one of moving from learning to doing. That means you should take command of the exercises, instead of sticking slavishly to the instructions. Do not hesitate to invent your own ways of doing them.

So, action:

Gaze

To look is certainly nothing exotic. Man trusts his vision more than any other means of perception, and uses it constantly, without reflecting much on it. But in the following, you will exercise another way of looking. I call it gazing, in order to distinguish it from regular looking. That is all I intend with my choice of word.

There are several different ways of looking, no doubt, and this has been noted for ages. It is marked by the many words used for the activity of the eyes, such as: watch, see, gaze, stare, observe, spot, glimpse, glance, ogle, eyeball, view, peep, peek, glare, and so on. Even more is implied with expressions like 'seeing through' or clairvoyance. Such grand perspectives are not applied here, but you will feel that a new way of looking emerges through this exercise. At least, it will give new clarity to whatever object you lay your eyes on.

氣

1   In this exercise you should sit or stand. If you lie down you see nothing but the ceiling, or the sky if you are outdoors, which is a bit monotonous. Apart from that, there is not much you need to consider.

2   Direct your head and your eyes toward an abject or a spot in front of you. Not something too near to you. The distance should be at least some ten feet, but as far away as possible is fine, as long as you can see the object clearly. Make sure that you know exactly what spot you are looking at, not just a large surface on which your eyes might start to wander.

3   Close your eyes and breathe calmly and deeply, focused on qi breathing – the flow in and out that is not air. Do this for a while before you move to the next step, so that you feel that you have a good qi flow going.

4   Commence a long exhalation through your nose and open your eyes *when your exhalation flows steadily* – but long before it ends. Look straight at the spot you had decided on, and continue breathing out. You can go on with the exhalation without air, described in the exercise to breathe in a square – but only if you feel that you can do it with conviction.

5   *Before the feeling of exhalation weakens,* close your eyes again. This is to avoid losing concentration, or landing

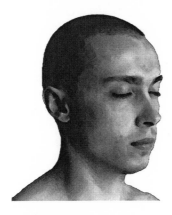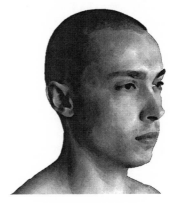

氣

on an unclear moment between exhalation and inhalation. It is important that you close your eyes while your breath still feels powerful.

6   Once is never. Take a few deep and calm breaths, and then repeat the exercise, exhaling and gazing at that spot anew. Remember to close your eyes before your exhalation weakens.

7   Continue as long as you feel that it gives you something. When you repeat the exercise, it will feel more and more like your exhalation goes through your eyes and all the way to the spot you aim at, as if your breath exits through your eyes and reaches that spot. The breath that travels this way is qi, of course. It makes you perceive the spot with a clarity that the eyes alone would not manage. It is as if you reach that spot, no matter how far away it is.

Contrary to regular breathing, qi can flow in any direction inside and outside your body. In this exercise, qi actually flows through your eyes and forward in the direction you look. When you have trained this more, it will feel like your gaze follows qi, not the other way around. It is as if your vision travels on the flow of qi. That gives a tangible quality to your gaze, as if you actually touch the thing you look at.

The eyes are passive tools that receive light and send impulses to the brain for interpreting. But qi is active, reaching the object.

One amusing way of training this kind of gaze is to do it toward animals – or past them. If you gaze right at an animal with your qi flow, you should not be surprised if the animal reacts – even if it is turned the other way. If you gaze past the animal instead, you will find that it does not react at all, even if it is very apprehensive. Be careful if you want to try this kind of exercise on an aggressive animal.

氣

氣

Point

This exercise is essentially identical to the former one. It is just another body part involved. Actually a combination of two: the eyes, like before, and the index finger. But the latter has the main role here. The role of the eyes is little more than to observe how the exercise works. They can also help to intensify the experience, as well as your ability to focus.

1   Just like in the previous exercise, you should stand or sit, but not lie down. Apart from that, there are no restrictions.

2   Aim at a spot in front of you – at least some ten feet away, but it works better if the spot you choose is far away. Make sure to decide exactly on a precise spot.

3   Close your eyes and start a good qi breathing. You should feel that the breathing and the qi flow work well, before you continue to the next step.

4   Begin a slow exhalation through your nose. Open your eyes when you feel that your exhalation flows steadily, and gaze right at the spot you have chosen.

5   Continuing your exhalation, extend your arm and point with your index finger at the spot. Your index finger should be aimed at the spot well before your exhalation

氣

ends. Continue to *point while you exhale.* You can continue also with the feeling of exhalation without air, described in the exercise on breathing in a square, if you can do that with conviction.

6 Before the feeling of exhalation weakens, close your eyes and lower your arm. It is important that you halt while your exhalation still feels strong.

7 Once is never. Take a few deep and calm breaths, and then repeat the exercise. Remember to halt before your feeling of exhaling weakens.

8 Continue as long as you feel that you improve, but interrupt immediately if your experience of the exercise weakens or gets vague. It should feel like you are breathing out through your index finger, in a flow toward the spot you aim at. That is qi flowing through your finger. When it feels as if the finger somehow reaches the spot, so that you can almost sense it on the tip of your finger, then you manage this exercise very well.

When you repeat this exercise it is good to choose different spots to aim at. Otherwise you might become too self-conscious, or you start doing it indifferently, like a routine.

Pointing is a simple and clear example of how qi relates to human action and perception. You gather your qi, thereby also your attention, in order to aim it in a specific direction or at a certain spot. Certainly, this is a form of concentration, but it is important to understand that it involves no strain or tension. This concentration is quite relaxed and natural. Still it is both effective and sharp.

You will notice that this way of fixing your eyes and finger on a specific spot makes you develop your mental ability to focus, to be concentrated on one thing at a time – without needing to strain yourself. You can also sort of point at more abstract or complex things, such as tasks and goals at work, actually even relations to other people. That way you can handle them with a clearer mind.

氣

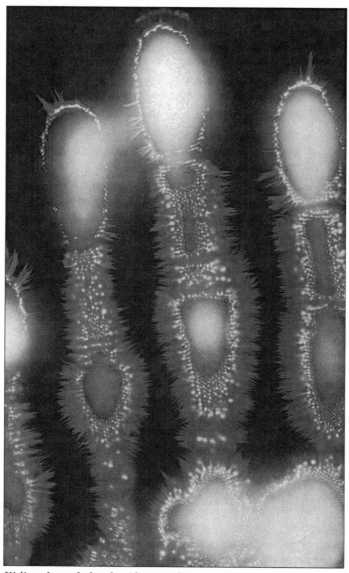

Kirlian photo of a hand, said to reveal its aura. This has been questioned by scientific examinations. The aura is a concept similar but not identical to that of qi.

氣

Push

The most amusing way of practicing pushing is by all the heavy doors we have to pass in everyday life – entrances to shops, elevators, apartment buildings, and so on. Any door with a spring to make it shut automatically is quite laborious to open. Passing through them, one after the other, can be turned into an excellent way of training the use of qi that I call pushing.

Here you use your qi flow to push doors open, but of course you can use the same method for any kind of pushing, whether it is an object, an animal, or a human being. Be careful, though, since your pushing might become more forceful than you expected.

1   Stand at about half an arm's length from the obstacle you want to push. When you are learning this, choose an object that is easy to give a push. A normal door without that spring construction to get it shut is sufficient to start with. Don't stand with your feet together, since that makes you unstable, but with one foot at least half a step in front of the other. Bend your knees slightly, which will also improve your balance.

2   *Don't aim at the obstacle, but past it*, in the direction you want to push it. This can be difficult if the object obstructs your view completely, like a door does. Still try to sort of look right through it, as if you had X-ray vision. In the beginning, the best is to exercise on a glass door, a garden gate, or some other obstacle that does not block your view.

3   Put the palm of your hand on the obstacle – the right one if you are right-handed, or the left if you are left-handed, so that you feel comfortable with your ability to push the object in a normal way. When you are used to this exercise, you can choose any hand. The palm of your hand should have good contact with the object, but not push on it yet.

4   Commence a powerful qi breathing from your lower

氣

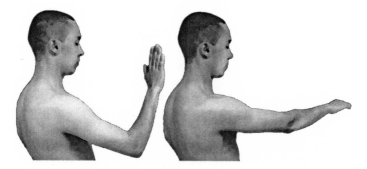

abdomen. You should feel that the breathing and the qi flow work well, before you continue.

5 Start a long exhalation through your nose. Look straight ahead – not at your hand, but way past it.

6 With a continued exhalation, shove your hand forward, so that you push away the obstacle. Do not think about the obstacle, but focus on the direction right past it. It should feel like you *breathe out through the hand* in a long exhalation that reaches far beyond the obstacle. The hand should sort of sail on this exhalation. Do not hesitate to increase the force of your exhalation while you are doing the actual pushing.

7 Make sure that you have pushed the obstacle away, before the feeling of exhaling weakens. It is important that you are finished with the pushing while your exhalation still feels strong.

8 Once is never. Take a few deep breaths, and then repeat the exercise.

9 Continue as long as you find it rewarding, but halt if you notice that you start to be sloppy with your breathing or your attitude in the pushing. As you have already understood, this exercise makes qi flow through your hand and give power to the pushing. Already at the first try you will find that your movement is more powerful than it would be without this method, and the obstacle is removed with greater ease than you expected. Be

氣

careful, because when you get good at this you can shove away quite heavy doors as if they were made of paper. You generate considerable power this way – much more than you originally estimated.

Pushing is just one example of how the qi flow can be used in just about anything you do. By using qi you get more power at your disposal. Even great exertions get much easier this way. The qi flow helps your muscles to work in unison and more efficiently, so you do get stronger than without this method – much stronger.

Also, there are lots of boring and tiresome tasks that become more fun and help you improve your way of working with your body. This joy in itself makes you feel better than you would if doing the same things without qi breathing. So, even at exertion you will have a greater amount of relaxation.

Go on and develop your own ways of getting things done with the help of qi breathing. Examine tasks that you often need to get done, and experiment with how you can use your qi flow in them. It can be used in most cases, although it sometimes takes clever thinking and adaptations to figure out the best way to go about it.

Pull

This exercise is the exact opposite of the pushing above. But opposites meet, so it is really just another way of working with the same powers. If you think in the pair of pushing and pulling, you should be able to find ways of using qi breathing in all kinds of tasks, no matter how complicated they might be.

The two directions of breathing – in and out – correspond to taking and giving, such as in pulling and pushing. That is why you pushed while breathing out in the former exercise, and in this one you should pull while breathing in.

Choose an object to pull that offers reasonable resistance. Something too heavy is not very encouraging to work

氣

on. Ideally, use a door with a closing spring, as suggested in the previous exercise – but this time one that opens to you, and not away from you. You can pull a normal door, too, but that is so easy you hardly feel it.

Another possibility is to use an elastic rope, like the ones used for fastening things to the roof rack of a car. Fasten one end in something stable, and grab the other end.

Observe that this is in no way body building. You do not need to pull that much or hard, for the exercise to do its good. It is enough that you feel some resistance. Thereby you are able to notice how your body works in the exercise.

1 You should really stand up, but if you find a suitable way of doing this exercise sitting down, this works as well. Make sure not to let your posture slope during the exercise.

2 The object that you will pull should be at almost arm's length distance from you, so that your arm is extended but not completely straight when you grab it. Belly height is to prefer, but not necessary. Use the right arm if you are right-handed, otherwise the left, so that you feel the strongest.

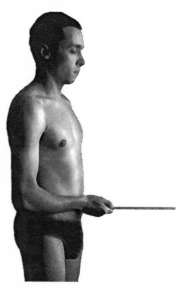

3 Commence qi breathing. You should feel that the breathing and the qi flow work well, before you move on.

4 Start a deep inhalation through your nose, and then pull the object to you. The best is if you can pull it directly toward your belly. It should feel as if you *suck the object to you* by inhal-

氣

ing. Therefore, your inhalation should feel as if it runs through the fist you grab the object with, and continues all the way to the bottom of your abdomen.

5   Release the object before your inhalation ends. Of course, if you work with an elastic rope you should do it carefully, with a peaceful exhalation.

6   Once is never. Calmly take a few deep breaths, and then repeat the exercise.

7   Continue as long as you feel that it gets easier to pull the object toward you. When it works as smoothly as a train moving on its track, then you are doing it well. If it starts to feel heavy or monotonous, you should stop. Then it has no more to give you, this time.

It is not always optimal to use the inhalation to pull things toward you, although it is the most natural way. For example, in tug-of-war the participants usually pant and moan, and make the most forceful pulls while exhaling. But upon closer examination there is actually no one pulling, at least not in the strict meaning of using the arms to get the rope closer to the body. Instead, they hold their arms at a fixed position, lean back, and push with their legs, which have the strongest muscles in the body. So, they use their legs to push, which is why they do right to exhale.

You are the strongest when you exhale – on the condition that you manage to do your task with a movement

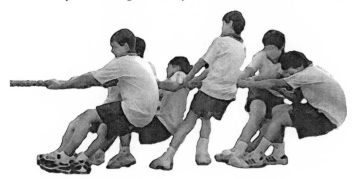

away from you, instead of toward you. Otherwise there is a contradiction between breath and body that diminishes the power.

The worst you can do is to hold your breath when doing something strenuous. Still, that is exactly what many people do, without thinking about it. They hold their breath as soon as they need to exert themselves. Check how you do, and correct it if needed. When you need power, make sure always to inhale with a spirit toward you, or exhale with a spirit away from you.

Grip

Holding something is strenuous for the simple reason that it is against nature. Life is movement and change, whereas that which is halted from moving comes closer to death. For that reason, there is always a measure of unease connected to holding something – and the unease increases while your grip remains.

The trick in grabbing something strongly and persistently is to do it with a feeling of movement – a flow instead of a halt. Qi breathing will accomplish that.

1   You can sit or stand, but avoid lying down in this exercise. Make sure that your posture is good.

2   Put the object you want to grip close enough for you to reach it comfortably. The best is to have it at about the same height as your belly. Practice with loose objects in the beginning, but later on you should be able to do it also on objects that are fastened. Choose an object with a smooth surface, so that you can grab it without discomfort.

3   Close your eyes and commence qi breathing. The breathing and qi flow should work fine before you move on to the next step.

4   Exhale and put your hand around the object you want to grip, but do not tighten the grip yet. Use your right hand if you are right-handed, otherwise your left, so

氣

that you feel the most able. When you have practiced this several times it does not matter that much what hand you choose. By then you do good to try both hands.

5   Start a long inhalation, and then tighten your grip on the object. Notice that you *grip while inhaling.* Most of the grip's force should be in your little finger. Actually, that is the only finger you need to focus on when you tighten your grip. The other fingers will do what they shall – neither more nor less. Because of your focus on the little finger, the angle of your fist will change a little. The side with your little finger will protrude slightly, and the thumb side will retreat correspondingly. It should feel like you *breathe in through your fist.*

6   Release the grip before your inhalation ends. When you have trained this some more, you can keep the grip longer by having a continued feeling of inhaling, although your lungs are filled with air. It is also possible to keep the feeling of breathing in when you exhale – but that takes some practice.

7   Once is never. Take a few deep and calm breaths, and then repeat the exercise.

8   Continue as long as you feel that it works well, without your body getting tense. It should feel like you suck the object to you, or even into you, with your inhalation. But keep your arm extended to avoid actually pulling the object toward you. On the other hand, if you really want to pull the object, you should do that, too, while breathing in.

氣

The nature of breath-
ing in is to bring things
toward you, whereas the
nature of breathing out is
to push things away from
you. Therefore you should
grip while inhaling, if you
want to keep the object
close to you or pull it toward you. Grip while exhaling if you
want to hold the object off or push it away.

If you grip while exhaling you will notice that the angle
of your fist will change in the opposite direction to the one
when you inhale. The thumb side of the hand will tilt
slightly forward, and the little finger side will move toward
you. Still, you should always focus on the little finger when
you grip something.

When you need to hold an object for long, grab it while
inhaling or exhaling, according to your intention: Use the
former if you want to hold it close to you, and the latter if
you want to keep it away from you. Then concentrate on
feeling like you breathe through your fist, both when inhaling and exhaling. You will notice that the grip remains
strong, without being that very straining.

But as I said in the introduction to this exercise: Holding something is basically against nature. Therefore it is
never that very restful or comfortable.

Walk

We move on with the exercises of extension – this time by
walking. Practicing qi extension on the most fundamental
body movements is excellent for developing your qi flow.

Initially, you have to repeatedly remind yourself of the
qi application when you do such unconscious things as
breathe, look, or walk. Without your conscious effort, you
are likely to forget all about qi and just behave as you have
done all the years up to now. But by time you will teach your
body and mind new habits, so that you will unconsciously

氣

work on the qi flow and extension no matter what you do. You practice qi without having to think about it. That is when the great rewards of it start to appear.

Walking with attention to qi is merely a continuation of the exercises with looking and pointing. You so to speak bring them outdoors. This really needs to be done outdoors, in the open air, with a clear view all the way to the horizon. Then there is room for your spirit to extend really far.

When you begin to work with this exercise, the free view can actually be a bit intimidating, because it feels too vast to be filled with your spirit. But this makes the exercise a challenge that you will soon learn to live up to. Once you have gotten over the reluctance to take your place in a vast space, and your spirit starts to expand over it, then you have a great inner movement going.

1   You should be outdoors. If you do this exercise indoors, choose something like a corridor, where you can see far ahead. Start by placing yourself so that you have a maximum of free space in front of you.

2   Look straight ahead, not exactly aiming at a certain spot, but sort of unfocused in the general direction. Therefore it is good if you have nothing special to aim at – not even the horizon, if it is visible.

3   Stand still and start a good qi breathing, preferably in the bottom of your abdomen, if you have learned to do so. Belly breathing makes you more stable, increases your balance, and gives you a stronger conviction when you start walking. While you breathe with qi, continue to look straight forward, without any other aim than the direction.

4   Commence a long exhalation through your nose. As soon as you feel that the ex-

halation is steady and flowing, walk forward in the direction you are looking. It is important that you do not start walking before your exhalation is steady. Otherwise your steps will also lack steadiness.

5   Continue to *walk forward as long as the exhalation feels steady and extended*. If you succeed in keeping this feeling even when you stop breathing air, you can go on walking.

6   Stop walking before your exhalation feels weakened. It is important that you only walk when your exhalation feels strong.

7   Take a few deep and calm breaths and repeat the exercise, by continuing to walk in the same direction. It should feel like *your steps ride on your exhalation*. You move forward by the power of your breath. What the feet do is of less importance. Remember to stop before your exhalation weakens.

8   Continue this kind of walking for a while. After some time you will not need to stop and take a few breaths, to recommence the qi flow. Just stopping shortly to inhale is enough. Soon you will be able to continue walking through the inhalations, too, without the stability of your flow and the strong sense of direction in your steps faltering.

This is a wonderful way of walking. By the extension of your breathing and your qi flow, it is a bit like a train on its track. Even a dull promenade through a neighborhood you have crossed far too many times gets exciting and invigorating. You will also notice how clearly you feel the ground

氣

under your feet, although that is not what you concentrate on. In addition, the air that you breathe will become particularly refreshing. All those good effects combined, you may find yourself walking much farther than you originally intended, from the pure delight of it.

This exercise can also be done running instead of walking, when you feel that you get the hang of it. But do not run so fast that you lose your breath and find it difficult to keep the extended exhalations.

氣

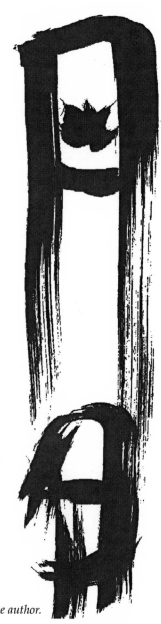

Dantian, the center. Calligraphy by the author.

氣

The Center

If you managed the previous exercises, you should by now have established a good posture, breathing, relaxation, and a fine flow of qi. So, now it is time to return to the very base of it all – the point that is the center of the life energy flow.

Of course, this center is involved in all the previous exercises, but I still believe that the proper order of introduction into these aspects is the one given in this book. Only after you have familiarized yourself with how to work on your posture, breathing, relaxation, and qi extension, is it time to concentrate on your center, although it is the most fundamental of all.

The reason for this order is that your perception of your center is far too vague, before you have commenced your flows. When you can feel your qi stream through and out of the body, then you can sense the center in which those flows have their origin. Beforehand, it would just make you confused if you tried to establish a sense of center.

Actually, in the Eastern perspective the center is far more than just a junction of your body's qi flows. It is the physical answer to the question: who am I? I am here, precisely in my center, a point of infinite exactness. From this precise point I act, and to this point I receive. Man's central station, if you like.

The previous exercises have shown clearly that this center is inside your belly, to be more precise a couple of inches below your navel – usually it is specified as three finger widths below the navel. It is with this point you should breathe, in order to commence a significant qi flow. So, it can be described as a center of power.

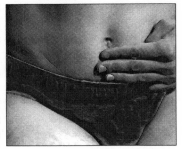

But this point in your lower abdomen is not the only possible center in your

氣

body. It is not that simple at all. There are seven points, which are usually counted from the bottom of the torso up to the top of the head:

1   the underside of the crotch

2   the belly, three finger widths below the navel

3   solar plexus, below the chest

4   the middle of the chest

5   the throat

6   the forehead

7   the top of the head, the fontanel

The Indian term for them is *chakra*, which originally means 'wheel'. This underlines their active and central function. It is an age-old tradition, which through the years has become so complex that it is almost impenetrable. I dare say that it is unnecessarily complicated, especially the way it is presented in the literature about it, and in all kinds of introductory systems taught to us poor westerners.

We do not need to make it that cryptic.

The seven chakras are spread through the body, but still connected, sort of like the 'connect the dots' drawings for children. But the figure that the chakras make when connected is the simplest one imaginable – a straight vertical line through the middle of the body.

There are illustrations that place the seven chakras here and there in the body, so that a line drawn through them would be a curve, slithering like a mountain road. That is not how I see it. The line is straight, running vertically through the body, and constitutes its fundamental pillar. The pil-

氣

lar of being. A tree of life, if you will, from which man's body and actions emerge like the branches of a tree.

This pillar is a mighty thing to get acquainted with. Qi should flow freely and forcefully through this pillar and all the seven chakras, when you have succeeded in opening yourself up properly. Then you become as stately as a temple.

It is beyond the scope of these exercises to go through all the seven chakras, their meanings and applications at depth. We settle with the chakra that the Eastern tradition regards as the basis for powerful qi breathing – the second one from the bottom, a couple of inches below the navel. But when you have learned to activate this point, you will discover that the other ones allow themselves to be awakened and developed, without too much trouble. That is how they are connected through the central line. If one point is stimulated, it makes the other ones come alive as well.

The second chakra is called *dantian* in Chinese, and *tanden* in Japanese. It is written with two pictograms. One of them means cinnabar red, and the other means rice field – so, the cinnabar red rice field. The red color is intense, like blood and fire. That the red color is linked to energy and life is no mystery – but what about the rice field?

Rice is the basic food for the Chinese and the Japanese. Since ancient times it has been the most important requirement for their survival. Rice brings power to their bodies, so a rice field represents a vast resource to promote and preserve life. This is the connection that explains why the sign for a rice field is used to describe the chakra we focus on.

Another connection to rice is found in the sign for qi, which has two parts combined into one pictogram – rice and steam. The boiling rice. Here too, rice is used to imply nourishment and an energy needed to sustain life.

Thereby it is obvious that the chakra we have chosen is particularly connected to qi. It is the source of the great flow

氣

of glowing life force. This also means that stimulating the qi flow automatically leads to stimulation of this chakra in particular. Naturally, this is mutual. Concentrating on this chakra in your body will lead to an enhanced qi flow.

In the beginning it is difficult to feel one's center clearly, therefore also to work with it. But this is true also for qi breathing, which is still stimulated by the previous exercises, without too much trouble. So, the same exercises are also good for increasing your perception of the second chakra.

This is particularly true for the following exercises:

1   meditation with your hands joined in front of your center

2   belly breathing exercises with your hand on your center

3   breathing in a square, with extended inhalations and exhalations, which do in their pure qi breathing phases activate your center considerably

4   exercises in pushing, pulling, and gripping, which involve your belly and your center in a physically concrete way

It is not easy to find exercises that directly stimulate your center, so to speak from inside of it instead of from the outside. Among the following exercises, some are modifications of previous exercises, focusing them on getting you to feel your center. Others are completely new.

So, how should your center feel? It is a point, infinitely exact, and therefore without any physical extension. But at the same time it sort of vibrates with potential, a force that can be brought forward. Maybe it should be compared to the black holes in space, containing so much in their formidable density that light itself is bent and swallowed by them. But your center can both swallow and erupt – with the same magnificence.

So, a strong sense of your center is of a point inside your body, which is of ghastly significance and makes its sur-

氣

roundings shudder by all that it is able to take and give. The actual center is like a black hole, the core of which cannot be perceived, but its surroundings are struck by a kind of trembling vibration, tickle or itch. That is what reveals the existence and potential of your center.

It seems almost unpleasant, as described above, but it still is both tempting and stimulating. It brings a feeling of immense ability and mystic grandeur that you will enjoy in spite of that odd itch.

Center breathe in a square

This is a small modification of *Breathing in a square*, which is one of the above breathing exercises. The simple difference is that this time you concentrate on the midpoint of qi breathing, your center in the lower abdomen, instead of focusing on prolonging your breath.

1   The best is to sit down with a good posture, or lie flat on your back, but do not stand up when doing this exercise. Wear loose clothing. No clothes at all is even better – at least none that covers your belly.

2   Put one hand on your belly with the middle of the palm on your center, three finger widths below your navel. The best is if the hand has direct contact with the skin on your belly, without anything covering it. Then put the other hand on top of the first one. You decide which one of the hands should be on top. Right-handed people might prefer to have the right hand closest to the body, and vice versa – but try both before you take it for granted.

3   Start a strictly regulated breathing with the same fixed time for each of its four phases: inhaling air, a continued feeling of inhaling without air, exhaling air, and a continued feeling of exhaling without air. Do not make the intervals too long. Settle for somewhere between five and ten seconds.

4   When you exhale, concentrate on how it feels inside the

氣

belly, under your hands. If you have not managed a good belly breathing before you do this exercise, you might not notice much at all, but with good belly breathing there is a distinct sensation. You feel power inside your belly, and sort of an itching at the core of your breathing – in your center.

5   Continue as long as it feels meaningful, while you sense *a point of power inside your belly*. You can go on as long as this feeling increases, but if it diminishes you should stop for now.

Because this exercise stimulates the qi flow considerably, and because you have your hands on the central area, your center will be evident to you. Of course, the more you make qi flow in your breathing, the more you will feel your center.

Even if you feel nothing special in your belly during this exercise, it still works as a stimulation of your qi flow and your belly breathing. And the next time you try it, you will surely feel more.

氣

Bodhidharma, the Buddhist monk who introduced Chan (Zen) to China. Woodprint by Yoshitoshi, 1887.

氣

Meditate the center

Here you use the meditation exercise from the chapter about posture to get a distinct sense of your center. The essence of meditation is really to think about nothing at all – at least in Zen – but in this case we still allow ourselves to use this method for another purpose, which is just as commendable.

It is also a clear feature of meditation, as of any form of spiritual stillness, that it allows you to perceive your body and its essence more closely than in other states of mind.

This exercise is rather abstract in nature and can be difficult to grasp, before you have any sense of your center. Therefore I recommend that you start with the previous exercise, the center breathing in a square, and stick with it until you get a clear result. Then it is time to try this one. It will enrich and deepen your experience.

1 Sit in the way described in the text about meditation, earlier in the book. You do not have to sit on the floor. A chair is fine too – if you can sit in it with a good posture. Unfortunately, that is difficult in most chairs. This time it does not matter much how you are dressed, as long as you do not wear clothes that are tight around your belly. You should feel comfortable, so that you are not distracted.

2 In this exercise you do best to close your eyes, since you should *turn your attention inward.*

氣

Therefore you need to lock out what is around you. Avoid letting your eyes turn upward inside your closed eyelids, because that tends to make you drowsy.

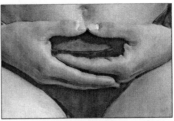

3   Make a closed figure with your hands, and have them rest in your lap, close to your belly or even touching it, in front of your center, about three finger widths down from your navel. The best is a figure that creates an opening in front of your center. Maybe the hands are too low if you let them rest in your lap. If so, bend your arms a little, so that your hands rise to the correct position. The important thing is to keep the opening that your hands create right in front of your center.

4   Breathe with your belly, using long and extended breaths that stimulate your qi flow. Enter the breathing with your mind, to be aware of its source in your center. The position of your hands makes this easier for you to perceive. They sort of create a frame around your center and thereby enhance your experience. Continue with the belly breathing, and do not bother about anything else than this breathing and its source.

5   When you succeed in fixing your attention on your center, it gives sort of a resonance all through your body, which makes your breathing particularly vitalizing. It is hard to keep your attention on your center all the time, but as soon as it is there you get this resonance, this sudden gush of inspiration. Even if you cannot describe it intellectually, this exercise will by time give you a deepened assurance of your center and its significance.

6   Sit as long as you can without getting uncomfortable. It does not have to be for very long – a few minutes can have a great effect. Whatever you experience during this time, you will surely find that subsequently you

have gained new energy, and you feel cleaner and clearer than before.

I know that this exercise is vague and almost incomprehensible by nature. But now we are dealing with the very essence of qi and its flow. This gets intangible. You will still be increasingly comfortable with the exercise, as you continue repeating it.

If you have tried this exercise a few times and still get no particular impression from it, although you belly breathe and your qi is flowing – then you can ignore it. In that case this exercise just isn't suited for you, so you spend your time better if you focus on other exercises in this book – those that give you more.

Sway

When fixing positions in the world around us – whether it is a ship's coordinates on the sea, or the distance to faraway stars in the Milky Way – we need at least two observation points. With readings from those two points it is possible to decide the position of a third one with great precision, even if it is very far away.

The same is true for the center in your body. You can fix its position by altering between two positions. The following exercise is a method to do just that.

So, the object of this exercise is to sort of calibrate the position of the center in your body, and then to settle right in this position.

1   Sit on the floor, preferably in the way described in several of the above exercises, with your legs underneath you. Otherwise it is difficult to keep your back straight. Sit on something soft enough for you to remain there comfortably for a while, but not so thick that you sink down in it and lose stability. Wear loose clothing, particularly around your belly and the whole area of your hips.

氣

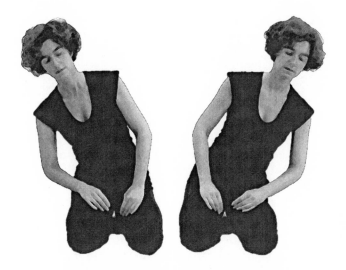

2 Breathe calmly and deeply, and make sure to keep a good posture. Let your hands rest on your thighs and relax. Also relax your arms. They should be passive. Close your eyes.

3 Start swaying to and fro, sideways. Try to sway in such a way that *the base of the movement is in your center*, three finger widths below your navel. Neither above nor below it. Make the swaying big in the beginning, moving far to the left and right – not so that you lose your balance, but not far from it. Do not bend your upper body or tilt your head this way and that. Your central pillar, the vertical line with your seven chakras, should remain straight.

4 Get into the swaying, sort of like you get lost in a song. You should feel like *a growing pillar*, all the way to heaven. It should really feel like you are growing, so that your swaying encompasses an increasing distance from side to side.

5 Without you having to think about it, the swaying of your body will slowly decrease, the bigger and more ex-

tended it feels to you. The angle of your swaying gets smaller and smaller. Do not control it consciously. Just let it happen. The higher up in the sky it feels like your central pillar reaches, the less your actual swaying of the body will be. Again: do not pay attention to it, just let it happen.

6   Finally, when you feel almost infinitely tall, as if your swaying reaches deep into the cosmos – then your body movement will stop completely. The feeling of swaying continues, but your body is still, in an absolutely vertical position.

7   Then let go of that swaying feeling, and allow your central pillar to sort of sink down in this vertical middle, like a spear shoved into the ground. Your central pillar, your straight posture, falls into place in the middle of your body. This is to sit down in one's center.

8   Connect your hands in a closed figure in front of your center. This way you seal the experience, and confirm that the exact position of your center has been established. Remain in this position for a couple of minutes or more, so that you are impregnated with its stability, and feel the certainty of it.

This is actually an exercise that you should not repeat immediately. It will not do any good. Instead, a repetition can lessen the experience as well as your ability to reach it again. Here, once is always – this time. You can try it again at another time.

This is an ancient exercise of Eastern origin. Once I was taught that the swaying should be done 360 times before you stop in the middle – a number that was in the past linked to the approximate number of days in a year, just like the number of degrees of a circle.

In my experience, though, you benefit from letting your feeling decide. When you reach the feeling of a growing central pillar and a posture that reaches heaven, then the swaying will diminish and stop by itself – no matter how many

氣

times you have swayed beforehand. This is a more natural and vivid way of doing it.

Press

An excellent way of getting acquainted with one's center is to use it. That is what you do in this exercise, even if you have not sensed it that clearly yet. It is a variation of the exercises in pushing, earlier in the book. This time you do not focus on the qi flow, but its origin – your center.

Still, you should use qi and the deep belly breathing, just like in the previous center exercises. It helps you to a more palpable experience, and an ability that reaches beyond what you expected to begin with.

1   Sit down at a little less than arm's length from a wall, or another solid vertical surface that you cannot move. A tree is even better, if you can practice outdoors. It gives a very lively experience. The best is to sit with your legs underneath you, like in the previous exercise, but if you can keep a straight back it is also fine to sit with your legs crossed in front of you. Avoid clothing that is tight around your belly.

2   Commence a deep and extended breathing, which includes a strong qi flow. Look at the wall in front of you, as if you wanted to see through it.

3   Put the palms of your hands on the wall, at about chest height. Make sure that you are close enough to the wall to reach it without having to extend your arms completely.

4   Begin a long exhalation, and press slowly on the wall with much force. It should feel as if your power comes from inside your belly, more precisely *from your center and straight toward the wall* – not via the shoulders, although that is where your arms are connected to your body. Both your exhalation and the hands pressing on the wall should feel like emanating directly from your

氣

belly onto the wall, without any roundabouts through your body.

5   If the pressure pushes your body backward, then you are doing it through your shoulders. If you are pressing from your belly, your center, it makes you *sit more steadily*, as if you were nailed to the floor. You may have to try it a few times before you get it right, but then you will notice that you just sit more steadily, no matter how hard you press your hands on the wall. Then you are doing it right – you are working from your center.

6   Stop pressing on the wall before the exhalation ends, and remove your hands. It is important that you do not work contrary to your qi flow, so stop before you switch to inhaling.

7   Take a few calm breaths and collect yourself, before trying it anew. You can repeat the exercise as long as you feel that you get better at it, or at least that you do it well, *without tipping backward*. Stop when you get tired or lose concentration.

氣

This exercise is quite effective for learning to work with your center, to fetch your power from it and thereby use your body resources in an optimal way. The exercise gives a clear impression of how your center functions, and exactly where it is situated, inside of you. In addition, it gives good balance and stability, physically as well as mentally.

This stability in body and mind is the primary mark of somebody being in touch with his or her center.

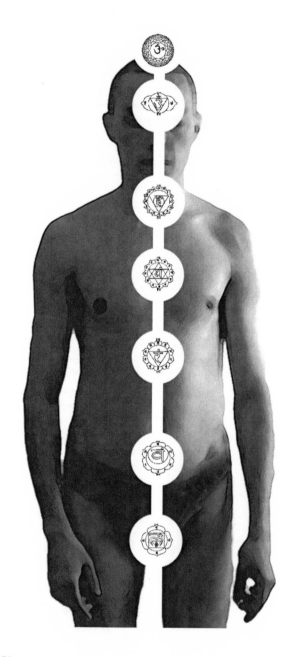

氣

Chakras

This book is primarily intended as one of practical exercises. Therefore, the facts and subject matter have been limited to what is relevant and necessary for the exercises. Still, there is good reason to mention something about the *chakras*, the Indian teaching about central points in the body. These have particular significance to the flow of qi, or *prana* as it is called in India.

For the purpose of what this book focuses on, there is an interesting practical side to the chakras: When you have familiarized yourself with qi and its point of power in your lower abdomen, you can experiment with the other points on your central pillar, make your qi breathing through any one of them, and feel what happens. Each has its own character, so you will notice that your experience varies according to what chakra you concentrate on in your qi breathing.

But you should regard this as extracurricular. The most important thing is that you calmly and methodically stimulate your qi flow with the basic methods presented above. Only when that works like a charm should you move on to try other chakras – maybe even work with the *kundalini* serpent, to get it slithering up your central pillar.

Yet I repeat: Wait with that until you have really anchored your qi breathing and a sense of a stable center. Otherwise you risk losing your stability and ability, instead of increasing them.

Seven chakras

Like all Indian traditional thought, the teaching about chakras is utterly extensive and complicated in its entirety. In addition, there are several contradictions in the literature about it, regarding just about everything from where these chakras are situated to their significance. Each chakra is usually linked to a color, an element, and one of the human senses, sometimes also a planet – but the books do not always agree about those matters.

In western tradition there are four elements, established by the old Greek philosophers: earth, water, air, and fire. These are used also for chakras, but with the addition of ether and light. The seventh chakra has no element of its own, but contains all or none of the previous six.

There is very likely a strong traditional link between the chakras and heavenly bodies, because that is the case in most of the ancient thought systems of the world. Apart from the comets, which appear and disappear, there are seven moving heavenly bodies in the sky that can be seen with the naked eye, and therefore have been observed all through history: the sun, the moon, Mercury, Venus, Mars, Jupiter, and Saturn. They should represent one chakra each, if there is any similarity between Indian tradition and those of other cultures.

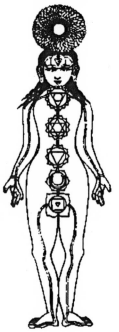

氣

Actually, as soon as you come across seven something in any ancient thinking, you can bet that it is based on the seven visual celestial bodies mentioned above. That is true for the seven days of the week, which are in many languages named after the planets, and for so many other elements of traditional thought.

As for colors, the western tradition has the spectrum of the rainbow and the prism, by Isaac Newton divided into a group of seven main ones: red, orange, yellow, green, blue, indigo, and violet. The colors connected to the chakras are not exactly the same, since both white and gold are included.

Regarding the human senses, there are five in the western tradition: smell, taste, sight, touch, and hearing. We sometimes talk about a sixth sense, which can be described as something akin to intuition. Indian tradition specifies the same senses, with the exception of the sixth, which is consciousness, and a seventh heightened one that we can call cosmic consciousness – maybe insight is a suitable word for it.

The central principle of *kundalini* is that man should awaken his chakras, from the bottom one and up, in order to realize his potential and bloom. Compare this to the lotus petals used in the symbols of the chakras, which are suddenly multiplied to a thousand at the seventh and highest chakra.

A symbol for this kundalini process through the chakras is the famous Indian mantra *Om* (or *Aum*), which can be uttered in a chanting way, so that it feels like the sound begins in the bottom of the abdomen, and gradually rises to the top of the head – through all the seven chakras. You start with sort of a belly push at the beginning of the word, so that it sounds approximately like A-U, which then slides over to O, rises through the body and becomes an M, vibrating in the skull when the lips are closed. It is an interesting exercise.

You can also familiarize yourself with any of your chakras by putting your hand or fingertip on it. This is an excellent way of perceiving them. It can be combined with exercises to breathe through the chakra where you have

氣

placed your hand. This is a good way of waking them up, one after the other.

Here are the seven chakras in the established order from the bottom to the top, and what they stand for:

1   Muladhara
Root
Lotus petals: 4
Color: red
Element: earth
Sense: smell
Planet: Saturn
Position: the bottom of the torso, pelvis

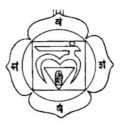

The first and lowest chakra is usually called the root chakra, which should also be understood as man's anchoring in physical existence – thereof the link to the element earth. The red color is not that easy to explain. Maybe it is originally associated to such basic components as the blood, which is the bodily fluid of life, and woman's menstruation.

It is not clear what planet belongs to this chakra – perhaps the red Mars, or the obscure and distant Saturn. What fits the best would really be Earth itself, which this chakra anchors us to. But in astrology it is rare to consider our planet as similar to the others, since that was not how it was seen in antiquity. They simply did not know that Earth below their feet is just another celestial body.

This chakra is where the kundalini serpent lies curled, before it is awakened and starts slithering up the central pillar toward the top. The chakra's position in the body should make it obvious that it concerns sexuality, but in most sources the second chakra has that role.

This is odd. No doubt, the root chakra must be essential in our sexuality, which can actually be used as a method to get the kundalini going. An orgasm that is felt from the lowest all the way to the seventh chakra is indeed excellent medicine for all the chakras.

氣

If you concentrate on the root chakra, preferably with the tip of one of your fingers in contact with it from below, you get a strong sense of being heavy and steady, and of being firmly rooted to the ground below your feet. It also makes you feel potent, able of creating the greatest wonder of all: life.

2   Svadhisthana
Dwelling of the I
Lotus petals: 6
Color: orange
Element: water
Sense: taste
Planet: Mars

Position: the belly, three finger widths below the navel

Enough about this chakra has been said in this book, which is practically devoted to it. The exercises above involve it, and have their beginning in it. This is the center for qi, the life force, the energy by which we get our strength and posture, act and accomplish. It is the dwelling of the I in the sense that the human body has its core and physical center of gravity here. So, it is the dwelling of the body's I, the bodily identity.

The chakra promotes integrity, self-trust, and personal ability. When it is awake and strong it chases away any sense of being lost.

Its element is water, maybe because of the liquids that the belly contains and processes. Its sense is taste – like in food, although that is something we actually perceive higher up in the body. Its color is orange, and its planet ought to be Mars, the powerful and martial, but some say Mercury.

Concentrating on this chakra, which is something this book has many exercises for, primarily gives a sense of growing power and capacity, almost animalistic in how natural and self-evident it feels. The energy that is possible to awaken here is so great that it can also awaken the chakra right below and the one immediately above. In Chinese and Japanese tradition, this is the chakra they almost solely focus on.

3 Manipura
City of jewels
Lotus petals: 10
Color: yellow
Element: fire
Sense: sight
Planet: Jupiter
Position: solar plexus

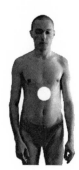

This is sometimes called the navel chakra, and might in past times have been placed there instead of in the solar plexus – or maybe it is just called so because of its vicinity to the navel. Most sources specify its color as yellow. Its element is fire, and its sense is sight, although the chakra is so far from the eyes. It might be the light of fire and of the yellow color that has led to its connection to sight. Also, things that we see and are affected by, can be felt the strongest in this area.

Its planet ought to be Jupiter, though some sources say the sun. But that extremely dominant celestial body must be reserved for the top chakra. It is given the name City of jewels because of the many good powers that radiate from here, according to the Indian tradition.

Putting your hand on this chakra is wonderfully soothing for the abdomen as well as for the whole body. It reinstates inner balances in the body, helps to cure different kinds of nausea, and stimulates relaxation. These good effects depend to a high degree on the fact that it is in this area that we tend to contract and get tense, when we are strained, stressed, or out of shape. Both physical and mental tensions tend to gather here, so this is where they can be dissolved.

氣

When you are out of shape, or tormented by one or other circumstance in your life, resting the palm of your hand on this spot is soothing indeed.

4 Anahata

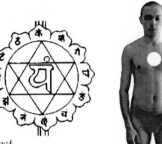

Unstruck
Lotus petals: 12
Color: green
Element: air
Sense: touch
Planet: Venus
Position: the middle of the chest

This being called the heart chakra simply depends on its nearness to the heart. Nor is it any mystery that the chakra is connected to the element air, since it is in the middle of the chest, where the lungs are.

Its sense is touch, which is easy to relate to for westerners. Also in our tradition the chest, and even more so the heart, is linked to feelings and emotions, which come near to what sensations touch brings. That Venus is the planet of this chakra is of no surprise to us. European astrology counts Venus as the planet of love, the foremost sentiment.

The color of the chakra is more difficult to explain. Some sources say that it is dark red, but that can very well be a western assumption, because of its link to emotions and love. Others say green – a color dealing with both harmony and subtle sensation. It is the color of vegetation, and thereby that of calm.

With the palm of your hand on this spot you can perceive the state of your emotions, and calm them down. It creates a certain level of inner peace, tranquility, maybe even happiness. It is like sadness and sorrow drain off, which can explain its name: unstruck. No one escapes unstruck by the harsh sides of life, but stimulating this chakra relieves quite a lot, as if it never happened.

5 Vishuddha

Pure
Lotus petals: 16
Color: blue
Element: ether
Sense: hearing
Planet: Mercury
Position: the throat

The chakra on the throat is connected to hearing, which is probably a consequence of the throat's ability to bring forth sounds. The same goes for its element ether, *Akasha* in Indian, which is what carries the sound. The color blue is not that easy to explain, if it is not the sky that is implied – the limitless ether, which seems to have a color, contrary to the air we breathe.

Both Jupiter and the moon are suggested as its celestial body, in literature about the chakras. I would vote for the former, if for no other reason so to save the moon for the next chakra, which it fits better. But Jupiter is already connected to the third chakra, so I would prefer to decide on Mercury for this one. That way, each chakra gets its own celestial body. Also, Mercury is closely related to speech and communication – at least in western astrology.

The purity that has given the chakra its Sanskrit name is diffuse. It might come from the neck being the border between the bodily and the mental, since it connects the torso to the head. Therefore, when the kundalini travels through this point it must do away with physical appetites and limitations.

Concentrating on this chakra is easy, even without putting your hand on it. It gives a sense of power, control, and the limitless ability of the will. With this force you can make decisions, choose between directions to go, and then stick to them. It is not advisable to make sounds concentrating on this chakra only. That becomes overly strained, forced, and loses a deeper resonance. Let us say that it is more the voice of the soldier than of the singer.

氣

6　Ajna

Command
Lotus petals: 2
Color: white
Element: light
Sense: consciousness
Planet: the moon
Position: the forehead

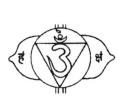

There are many suggestions about what heavenly body belongs to this chakra. Some say Saturn, others Jupiter, but most of the literature on the subject says the moon. It is also supported by several strong arguments.

From a purely astrological perspective, the moon should have this elevated position, since it is only surpassed by the sun. Also, it suggests the color white, which is the one most often linked to this chakra. Some suggest indigo, but that would be the Newton spectrum speaking. White and silver belong to Ajna – and to the moon.

Its element is said to be light. That, too, argues for the moon as its celestial body, because it is the second brightest light in the sky. The human sense ruled by this chakra is consciousness, the thinking man's ability to ponder himself as well as his surroundings. Western astrology sees the moon as representing the subconscious, which is close enough. The Indian tradition does not make the same distinction between the conscious and the subconscious, since it mainly aims for a higher, transcended consciousness.

The chakra commands in the same was as the conscious mind rules the body – more or less successfully. In the west we speak about the third eye, which we place at the same spot in the forehead, but this is not something from the Indian tradition. Still, there are some obvious parallels. To see through, understand, and realize, are significant for the third eye as well as for this chakra.

You can concentrate on this point by putting the tip of one of your fingers on it. This immediately gives your breathing a sparkling, inspired quality. Your whole head gets

氣

a resonance, which fills you with inspiration and spiritual clarity. Were it not for the tendency of this kind of breathing to sort of exclude the body, it would be excellent for practicing qi breathing. But you need to involve the body, in order to make of yourself a harmonious whole. Still, Indian breathing exercises are often focused on this chakra.

7   Sahasrara

Thousand petaled
Lotus petals: 1000
Color: gold
Element: all/none
Sense: cosmic consciousness
Planet: the sun
Position: the top of the head

The seventh chakra is in some traditions placed on the top of the skull, and in some right above it – that is outside the body. This is the chakra that connects man with the heavenly, the great cosmos, and therefore the last step in the kundalini emergence. It is called the crown chakra, and its symbol is a lotus with a thousand petals, which should be understood as an image of infinity.

This concluding chakra belongs to the limitless and the eternal. Its color is gold, of course, shining with the brilliance of a million suns. It encompasses all elements, or none, and it is connected to all of our senses – but mostly it points to the fully enlightened human being, with the consciousness of a cosmic nature, bringing us in contact with the gods.

There are varying reports on what planet the chakra is linked to. Some say *Ketu*, the Indian name for the moon's south node, but the only plausible choice according to astrological reason must be the sun. In ancient times, it was the sun that inspired the ideas of this chakra.

It is difficult to get a clear impression when concentrating on this chakra – to no surprise, since it is the final step

氣

in a long process through the previous six chakras. It helps to put a fingertip or the palm of your hand on this spot, the fontanel at the top of your head. But do it very lightly, so that you hardly touch it – since this chakra is partly outside the body, and incorporeal indeed.

What you can feel is a sudden rising, as if you started to grow toward the sky, or began to levitate upward. Well, you can come to feel a lot more – but that is personal, something for you to discover on your own spiritual quest.

Still, do not foster the idea that there is a shortcut. Working on only this chakra will not awaken the six below. Without them, your progress will be illusionary, lacking the base that makes your body a functioning vessel for the ascendance of your spirit. For that, it is better to start from the root. A tree cannot grow from its crown down.

Yin and yang, the opposites that make a whole.

氣

Quick Guide

When you have worked through all the exercises in this book, it will surely be unnecessary for you to reread the elaborate descriptions of them, next time you exercise. Not to waste your time, you find a quick guide on the following pages, with very short descriptions of every exercise. You can use it until you have memorized them.

Before you really feel that you do it right and make the progress you can expect, it is still good to have a look at the elaborate descriptions of the exercises above, occasionally. Otherwise there is a risk that you are mistaken about some detail, spending your time and effort on faulty or flawed exercises that are not as helpful as they should be. If you do an exercise incorrectly for a long time, you might even establish faulty habits that are very difficult to do away with later on.

The risk of mistakes is not big, since these exercises are so simple and basic. Nonetheless, pay attention to the details. If you accidentally get something this basic wrong, it will confuse your body and lead your intuition astray.

氣

So, when you are learning the exercises: shift between the extensive explanations above and the short descriptions below. You will know when you have learned them well enough to stick to the quick guide only. Later on, it is time to put this book on the shelf for good.

Exercises
Posture 135
Find the right posture
Correct your shoulders
Adjust your balance
Stretch your posture
Sit
Meditate
Relaxation 137
Clench and open
Shoulders up and down
Grimace
Empty gaze
Huddle up
Hang
Rest heavily
Breathing 139
Extend your exhalation
Lower your breath
Belly breathing
Breathe in a square
Extension 140
Gaze
Point
Push
Pull
Grip
Walk
The center 143
Center breathe in a square
Meditate the center
Sway
Press

氣

Posture

Find the right posture

1. Lie straight on the floor.
2. Rest for a moment.
3. Get up slowly.
4. Stand in the position your body had when lying down.
5. Remain there for a moment.
6. Repeat a couple of times.

Correct your shoulders

1. Stand straight.
2. Extend your arms horizontally. Point far away, in both directions.
3. Let the arms fall to the sides, without changing the position of the shoulders.
4. Remain there for a moment.
5. Repeat once or twice.

Adjust your balance

1. Stand straight.
2. Rise on your toes.
3. Sink down on the soles again, with the same posture.
4. Repeat as much as you like.

Stretch your posture

1. Stand straight.
2. With an extended inhalation, stretch your arms over your head, get up on your toes, and look straight up.

3   With a strong exhalation, stretch even more up-
    ward.

4   Go down to the initial position, before breathing
    in.

5   Breathe normally and relax.

6   Repeat a couple of times.

Sit

1   Stand straight.

2   Sit down on your shinbones, with your palms on your
    thighs. The upper body should have the same posture
    as when standing up.

3   Lift your upper body straight up, and then
    sink down again.

4   Press your knees together, until they are
    one fist apart.

5   Stand up straight.

6   Repeat once or twice.

Meditate

1   Your head should be angled so that it has the rear fon-
    tanel as its highest point.

2   Your eyes should be almost closed, gazing at the floor
    about one meter ahead. Lips closed. The jaws should
    not be pressed together. The tip of the tongue should
    touch the roof of your mouth lightly.

3   The hands are brought together to a closed
    figure.

4   Belly breathe, and think of nothing.

5   Sit as long as you can, without discomfort.

6   In meditation, you are in the middle of your
    center.

氣

Relaxation

Clench and open

1 Stand or sit. Close your eyes.

2 Clench your fists as hard as you can, together with inhaling through your nose.

3 Open your hands, together with a sudden exhalation through your mouth.

4 Repeat, as long as it makes a difference.

Shoulders up and down

1 Stand or sit, preferably with closed eyes.

2 Pull up your shoulders, together with inhaling through your nose.

3 Let the shoulders fall, together with a sudden exhalation through your mouth.

4 Repeat, as long as the shoulders get more relaxed.

Grimace

1 Stand or sit.

2 Grimace with your whole face, together with inhaling through your nose.

3 Relax your face, together with a sudden exhalation through your mouth.

4 Repeat a couple of times.

Empty gaze

1 Stand, sit or lie down, where you have an open sight in front of you.

2 Close your eyes hard, together with inhaling through your nose.

3   Open your exes, together with a sudden ex-
    halation through your mouth. Don't focus
    your gaze on anything particular.

4   Repeat several times.

Huddle up

1   Sit in a squatting position, preferably with closed eyes.

2   Embrace your legs and press them to your chest, to-
    gether with inhaling through your nose.

3   Extend slowly, until you lie straight on
    the floor, together with a long exhala-
    tion through your mouth.

4   Rest in this position for a moment.

5   Repeat.

Hang

1   Stand up.

2   Heave yourself up, so that the feet lose contact
    with the floor.

3   Hang for a while and breathe calmly. Wiggle
    your feet and swing your hips slightly.

4   Stop when it is too straining on your arms. Re-
    peat after a short pause.

Rest heavily

1   Lie straight, with closed eyes.

2   Take a few deep breaths, with pauses between them.

3   Accept and enjoy gravity.

4   Lift one hand a bit from the floor, and let it fall.

5   Lift the whole arm, a leg, or all arms and legs at the
    same time. Let them fall. Lie still and accept your
    weight on the floor.

氣

6   For each breath – especially the exhalations – you should feel an increased weight.

7   Feel yourself sink deeper into the floor, by your weight and by accepting the force of gravity.

Breathing

Extend your exhalation
1   Stand, sit or lie down.

2   Breathe in through your nose.

3   Exhale through your mouth, as long as possible, and then some more.

4   Close your mouth and let the inhalation happen automatically.

5   Open your mouth and exhale like before.

6   Repeat. Keep your posture.

Lower your breath
1   Stand, sit or lie down.

2   Breathe normally for a moment.

3   Place the palm of your hand on your lower abdomen.

4   Commence a slow exhalation through your nose.

5   Give your palm a push, only by a sudden exhalation.

6   Repeat until it works well.

Belly breathing
1   Walk, stand or lie down.

2   Place the palm of your hand on your lower abdomen.

3   Inhale through your nose, so that your belly pushes on your hand.

4 Exhale through your mouth – also so that your belly pushes on your hand. At both inhalation and exhalation, your belly seems to be expanding.

5 When it works well, take away your hand, but continue with the same breathing.

6 If it is mostly your chest moving, put your hand back on your lower abdomen.

7 Continue as long as you like, without getting tense.

Breathe in a square

1 Sit or lie down.

2 Breathe through your nose.

3 Start a regulated breathing, with exhalation and inhalation taking the same time.

4 After inhaling, add the same time with a continued feeling of inhaling.

5 After exhaling, add the same time with a continued feeling of exhaling.

6 Now, you're breathing in a square. Continue as long as it feels rewarding.

7 The feeling of inhaling and of exhaling – that is qi.

Extension

Gaze

1 Sit or stand.

2 Aim at a spot far away.

3 Close your eyes and commence qi breathing.

氣

4   With a long exhalation through the nose, open your eyes and gaze at the spot.

5   Before the exhalation weakens, close your eyes.

6   Repeat.

7   Continue as long as it gives you something.

Point

1   Sit or stand.

2   Aim at a spot far away.

3   Close your eyes and commence qi breathing.

4   Start a long exhalation through the nose, open your eyes and gaze at the spot.

5   With a continued exhalation, extend your arm and point at the spot.

6   Close your eyes and lower the arm, before the exhalation weakens.

7   Repeat.

8   Continue as long as it works better than before.

Push

1   Stand steadily about half an arm's length from the object you want to push.

2   Aim past the object.

3   Place the palm of your hand on the object.

4   Commence powerful qi breathing.

5   Start a long exhalation through your nose.

6   Extend your hand and push the object away. It should feel like you exhale through your hand.

7   Before the exhalation weakens, you should have pushed the object away.

8   Repeat.

9   Continue as long as it gives you something.

Pull

1   Stand or sit.

2   The object you want to pull should be at a little less than arm's length distance.

3   Commence qi breathing.

4   Start a long inhalation through your nose, and pull the object to you. It should feel like you suck in the object to you with your inhalation.

5   Release before your inhalation weakens.

6   Repeat.

7   Continue as long as it gets easier than before.

Grip

1   Sit or stand.

2   The object you want to grip should be at no more than half an arm's length away.

3   Close your eyes and commence qi breathing.

4   Exhale and put your hand softly around the object.

5   With a deep inhalation, grip the object, with the most power in your little finger. It should feel like you inhale through your fist.

6   Release before the inhalation weakens.

7   Repeat.

8   Continue as long as it works fine, without you getting tense.

氣

Walk

1 Stand where you have a clear way ahead.

2 Direct your gaze straight-ahead, unfocused.

3 Commence qi breathing.

4 With a long exhalation through your nose, walk forward.

5 Walk as long as the exhalation is stable.

6 Stop before the exhalation weakens.

7 Repeat. It should feel like your steps ride on your breathing.

8 It is fine to continue for a good while.

The Center

Center breathe in a square

1 Sit or lie down.

2 Place your hands on your center.

3 Breathe in a square, with the same time for inhalation, the continued sense of inhaling, exhalation, and the continued sense of exhaling.

4 Concentrate on how it feels in your belly.

5 Continue as long as you want, while you feel a power point in your belly.

Meditate the center

1 Sit like in meditation.

2 Close your eyes. Do not let your eyeballs turn upward.

3 Bring your hands together into a closed figure, resting in front of your center.

氣

4   Feel the source of your breathing in your center.

5   When you focus on your center, it gives a resonance all through your body, making your breathing significantly more vitalizing.

6   Sit as long as you can, without getting uncomfortable.

Sway

1   Sit, preferably with your legs under your body.

2   Breathe calmly and deeply, with your hands on your thighs. Eyes closed.

3   Sway with your whole upper body from side to side, with the base in your center.

4   Let your mind enter into the swaying, with the feeling of a growing pillar.

5   Your body's actual swaying diminishes, the bigger you make it feel.

6   Finally, your body movement stops completely, in a precisely vertical position, although the feeling of swaying continues.

7   Let go of the swaying feeling, and let your central pillar sit in this vertical middle. This is to sit in one's center.

8   Bring your hands together into a closed figure, resting in front of your center. Remain in this position for a minute or two.

Press

1   Sit at less than arm's length from a wall.

2   Commence deep qi breathing. Look at the wall in front of you, as if gazing right through it.

氣

3   Put the palms of your hands on the wall, at about chest height.

4   Commence a long exhalation and press slowly, but with force, on the wall. Your force should come from inside your center and straight at the wall.

5   If your upper body is pushed back, you are pressing from your shoulders. If you press from your center, you will sit more steadily.

6   Remove your hands from the wall, before your exhalation weakens.

7   Repeat as much as you like, as long as you don't get tired.

氣

Breinigsville, PA USA
05 March 2010
233685BV00001B/24/P